Game Night
In Buffalo

A Town, its Teams and its Sporting Memories

Written By
Sal Maiorana
©2003

©2003 Western New York Wares Inc.
All rights reserved.
Printed by Petit Printing
Layout and Design by Gracie Mae Productions

Address all inquiries to:

Brian Meyer, Publisher
Western New York Wares Inc.
P.O. Box 733
Ellicott Station
Buffalo, NY 14205
e-mail: buffalobooks@att.net
Web site: www.buffalobooks.com

This book was published and printed in Buffalo, NY
ISBN: 1-879201-44-5

Contents

Acknowledgements

While I conducted many personal interviews for the writing of this book, and I either attended as a fan or covered in my job as a sports writer for the Rochester Democrat and Chronicle some of these events, much of the information was culled from accounts in newspapers, magazines and books.

To that end I extend a hearty thanks to the following sports writers whose prose I referenced in the re-creating of these stories: Leo Roth, Scott Pitoniak, Bob Matthews, Gary Fallesen, Vic Carucci, Jim Kelley, Mark Gaughan, Bucky Gleason, Milt Northrop, Jerry Sullivan, Allen Wilson, Larry Felser, Bob DiCesare, Tom Borrelli, Mike Harrington, Donn Esmonde, Budd Bailey, Jim Peters, Dick Johnston, Ross Brewitt, Tony Violanti, Mike Billoni, Chuck Ward, Mike Abdo, Bob Davies, Chuck Pollock, Mike Vaccaro, Cy Kritzer, Ray Ryan, Charley Bailey, Bob Powell, Phil Ranallo, Charley Young, W.S. Coughlin and Joe Alli.

In the procurement of photographs I must thank Mike Groll for his dazzling cover shot as well as freelance photographer Robert L. Smith, Mike Gilbert and Bill Wippert of the Buffalo Sabres, Tom Burns of the Buffalo Bisons, Marc Gignac of Canisius College, Steve Mest of St. Bonaventure University, Jeff Ventura of Buffalo State College, Garry Dunlap of Niagara University, Shawn Dowd, Annette Lein, Wil Yurman and Jamie Germano of the Rochester Democrat and Chronicle, and Mary Karen Delmont at the Butler Library at Buffalo State College.

Special thanks to two entities: To Brian Meyer, Tom Connolly and Michele Ratzel of Western New York Wares, Inc., for the outstanding work they do in publishing books that relate solely to Buffalo and Western New York. They have carved a unique and much-needed niche in the local marketplace, and I am thankful to now be included amongst their fine stable of publications; And to the folks at Empire Sports, particularly Bob Koshinski, for allowing me a venue to originally publish the majority of these stories on their website, Empiresports.com. This book is a collection of the best columns that have run, or will run in the future, on the Empire website under the heading Maiorana's Memories.

Finally, I must thank my wife, Christine, whose undeterred love and support allows me to pursue my passion for writing, and my children, Taylor, Holden and Caroline, for the sheer joy they bring to my life and for their willingness to share their daddy with the computer.

Publisher's Ponderings

When Sal Maiorana contacted me in early 2003 about publishing his new book on banner moments in Buffalo sports history, I found myself wandering down memory lane.

His inquiry transported me back to a night in 1991 aboard a Holland America cruise ship. It was Super Bowl Sunday, and it sure seemed like we were the only Buffalo Bills fans aboard an ocean liner crawling with New York Giants diehards. We watched in stunned disbelief as Scott Norwood's 47-yard field goal attempt sailed wide right with only seconds left in the game. Even the gluttonous midnight buffet couldn't lift our sunken spirits.

Sal's pitch reminded me of my teen-aged years, when my dad would take me down to the Old Rock Pile for Sunday afternoon games. And of my first Buffalo Braves outing with a school buddy from St. Joe's. I felt like a tycoon as his parents treated us to a pre-game feast in the Aud Club.

I recalled my days as a radio reporter, covering the long-awaited opening of Pilot Field. A decade later, I would track crews' progress as they built a new downtown hockey arena. Attending my first Sabres' game in what was then Marine Midland Arena took on special meaning as I reflected on the years of planning – and wrangling – that went into the project.

This tidal wave of memories was proof enough for me that Sal had a winning concept. After all, sports has touched the lives of most Western New Yorkers in one way or another. *Game Night in Buffalo: A Town, its Teams and its Sporting Memories* serves up something for everyone. And you don't even have to be a sports diehard to enjoy this collection of revealing anecdotes.

No book project is a one-man show. Publishing is a lot like sports. Success requires team-work. Our thanks to Business Manager Michele Ratzel who has been a key player since the early 1990s. Tom Connolly, our marketing manager, has been equally instrumental in helping our company to grow.

We also thank the entire crew at Petit Printing and graphic artist Scott Kropidlowski of Gracie Mae Productions for their fine efforts.

On a personal note, I thank my friend Lawrence Peita, a Buffalo native and sports diehard, for serving as a valuable "sounding board" for so many of our publishing ventures over the years. Hang in there, buddy.

Brian Meyer
Founder and Publisher

Introduction

For 11 years Steve Tasker listened to the guttural roars of sellout Rich Stadium crowds, and he bathed in the waves of noise and adoration that cascaded down upon he and his Buffalo Bills teammates.

"The place was unbelievable," Tasker recalled of the glory years when the Bills were going to Super Bowl after Super Bowl after Super Bowl after Super Bowl and taking their legion of fans on the sporting ride of a lifetime. "It was loud in that stadium, really loud, a force. I remember the playoff games we had that were unlike anything I've ever seen because the crowd was absolutely a major part of the games."

Tasker and Jim Kelly, Thurman Thomas, Bruce Smith, Andre Reed, Kent Hull, Darryl Talley and all the other Bills reveled in the amorous attention, and they repeatedly lauded the fans who lauded them. But while they were proclaiming Buffalonians to be "the greatest fans in the world" there was always an undeniable disconnection because as players, they couldn't quite relate to the depth of the fans' passion. They could see it in their contorted faces, hear it in their hoarse voices, and ultimately they could use it to their emotional benefit on the field. But could they honestly understand it?

"Even in those magic years when we were going to the Super Bowls and we had those phenomenal runs and those historic moments, we were so focused on the games and our jobs and playing and winning, we didn't fully realize the magic that was going on with the team and the fans," Tasker said. "What a special time, and we didn't see the magic then. We felt it, and we certainly reaped the benefits from it, but we were too focused to step back and say 'Wow, this is really cool.'"

It wasn't until a couple of years after Tasker retired when he realized just how "cool" it was, and he truly grasped how devoted the fans of Buffalo are to the Bills, and to varying degrees, the Sabres, Bisons, Bandits, Destroyers, the defunct NBA Braves, and the local college basketball teams.

It was a cold November morning and Tasker's son, Luke, needed to sell candy bars to raise money for his youth hockey team. Tasker decided to take Luke over to the stadium parking lots prior to a Bills game figuring there would be thousands of willing customers. Luke sold plenty of candy bars that day, and his father, at long last, came to understand the fervency of fandom in Buffalo.

"We went across Abbott Road over into the ECC parking lot, and I was absolutely blown away," Tasker remembered. "It was like the apocalypse. People camping out, people with their bodies painted, parties of 200 people all wearing matching shirts, parties of two people. There were vans, campers, bonfires, $3,000 grills. There was smoke and fog and cold. I couldn't believe it. You stand up on the flatbed of a truck and you look out and it seems endless. It just struck me what an atmosphere there is on game day, and we as players didn't get to see that. Like I said, I was blown away."

Tasker was not the first, nor will he be the last, professional or amateur athlete to be "blown away" by Buffalo's knowledgeable, hearty sports fans.

Billy Shaw, the Pro Football Hall of Famer who played offensive guard for the Bills during their AFL days in the 1960s, once said "I thoroughly, thoroughly enjoyed my career in Buffalo. I was lucky I went there. The city, the fans, they put their arms around me as an individual and my family. I wouldn't change that for anything in the world. I couldn't imagine playing anywhere else. I couldn't imagine not being a Bill."

Rick Lancellotti, who played just one full season in Buffalo as a member of the baseball Bisons, was born in Concord, N.H., grew up in New Jersey, and played pro ball in seven countries on four continents spanning 17 years. Magellan had nothing on this world traveler. Yet despite everywhere he's been and everything he's seen, one of the most memorable years Lancellotti ever spent was 1979 in Buffalo, the year professional baseball returned to Buffalo after a nine-year absence. That season he cranked 41 home runs and became a hero to the War Memorial Stadium patrons, and so touched was he by the reception he received from Buffalonians that when he finally ended his baseball odyssey and retired, he became a Buffalonian.

"Up until the time I came here I hadn't felt that closeness that people have for each other," Lancellotti said. "When you think of all the places I played, including Hawaii, and here I am, married to a Buffalo girl, living in Buffalo, owning my own business in Buffalo. The people are great."

Randy Smith grew up on Long Island and came to Buffalo to attend college at Buffalo State in 1967. Smith had never even heard of the campus on Elmwood Avenue, and as a down-stater had barely acknowledged the existence of Buffalo until he came here to participate in a state high school track meet. By the time he left town more than 11 years later he had fallen in love with the city, its citizens, its sports fans.

Smith was an All-American athlete in three sports at Buffalo State, and upon graduation was drafted by the Braves, Buffalo's NBA team that had a sadly-too-short life span of eight years. Smith became an instant favorite at Memorial Auditorium because the fans considered him one of their own. In a way, they adopted him.

"I remember thinking it wasn't a bad move leaving Buffalo to go out to San Diego," Smith said, recalling the Braves' relocation to the West Coast following the 1978 season. "But then I got out there and yeah, the weather was great, but after those Buffalo years it was never the same for me. They (fans in San Diego) didn't appreciate me and the rest of the Braves like they did back in Buffalo. Once I got to San Diego and the other cities I played in, it made me realize how special it was in Buffalo and how important the teams are to Buffalo."

I can vouch for that importance. Long before I became a sports writer who vowed to uphold the time-honored journalistic standard of being an unbiased purveyor of information, I was a dyed-in-the-wool Buffalo sports fan. Born at Buffalo's Children's Hospital in 1962 I grew up rooting for the Bills, the Sabres, the Braves, the baseball Bisons and the local college basketball teams.

I sat in the rickety wooden seats at War Memorial Stadium watching the Bills at a time when people thought O.J. Simpson was going to be a bust as a football player but off the field would be a wonderfully charismatic and decent human being. And nearly a decade after I assumed I'd seen my last event at the old Rockpile, the city slapped a few hundred gallons of paint on the old lady and I was back watching the Bisons when baseball returned in Double-A form to Buffalo. I even worked for the Bisons part-time for a brief spell – if I'm not mistaken, I was not paid – and during that time I took a whirl behind the microphone as the public address announcer and operated the scoreboard for a few games.

My dad and I attended the very first game at Rich Stadium in the summer of 1973 when Herb Mul-key of the Washington Redskins returned the opening kickoff 103 yards for a touchdown and we thought, geez, only in Buffalo could that have happened. I later became a frequent visitor to Rich in the late 1970s and throughout the 1980s, transitioning into 1990 when I traded in the cold aluminum benches for a cozy seat up in the press box as I became a full-time Bills beat reporter for the Rochester *Democrat and Chronicle.*

The Aud was probably my favorite hangout. I remember creeping to the edge of my seat to watch Gilbert Perreault on one of his exhilarating end-to-end rushes up the ice, or he and his French Connection linemates, Rick Martin and Rene Robert, dazzling opposing teams with their flair and skill. I can vividly recall Bob McAdoo's unique leg kick when he let fly with a 20-foot jumper, and the amazing accuracy of Ernie DiGregorio's behind-the-back passes and free throws. I can remember the trilogy of Little Three basketball – Canisius, Niagara and St. Bonaventure – waging holy wars against each other, usually in games that meant nothing on a national scale, but meant everything to Western New Yorkers. I even watched the old Buffalo Stallions play indoor soccer in that place and can admit that I remember a Stallion named Lajos Ku.

"Sports is part of the culture here," said Tasker, a native of Kansas who has forged his life-after-football in Western New York, who has become a Buffalo sports fan, and who admits that one of the greatest sporting moments he has ever witnessed did not occur in one of the games he played as a Bill, but was Derek Plante's overtime goal in Game 7 of the Sabres' playoff victory over Ottawa in 1997. "People really take a great sense of pride in having sports up here that they can be proud of."

People like you. People like me. People like Tasker.

Of course, the Buffalo sports fan has much to be proud of, and that's what this book is about.

These pages are a celebration of sports in Buffalo. They bring to life the excitement the teams have provided, they accentuate the glory of their victories and reveal the heartbreak of their defeats, and they illuminate the athletes who have proudly worn Buffalo's uniforms. Ultimately, these pages allow us to relive the games we have never forgotten, the games that have shaped Buffalo's sporting culture.

Since their inception in 1960 when Detroit businessman Ralph Wilson purchased an expansion team in the fledgling American Football League and picked Buffalo to be his home base, the Bills have been Buffalo's showcase team. "For football, Buffalo is the perfect city," Wilson once wrote in *The Buffalo News*. "The fans here understand the game better than those in many other towns."

What a journey the Bills have taken us on. From the back-to-back AFL championships in 1964 and 1965, to the merger with the NFL which vaulted Buffalo into the big time, to the drafting and ultimately record-breaking success of Simpson, to the playoff excitement of the early 1980s, to the unprecedented feat of appearing in four straight Super Bowls in the 1990s, to the current rebuilding program being shepherded by Tom Donahoe, and all the down times in between, the Bills have commanded our undivided attention. Buffalo has had the privilege of being entertained by Hall of Fame players such as Simpson, Shaw, Kelly, Joe DeLamielleure and James Lofton, as well as other all-time greats such as Tasker, Smith, Reed, Thomas, Talley, Hull, Jack Kemp, Cookie Gilchrist, Tom Sestak, Mike Stratton, Joe Ferguson, Fred Smerlas, and we were enlightened by the wisdom of another Canton, Ohio enshrinee, coach Marv Levy.

And then there are the games. Oh, what games they have been.

There are seven included in this collection: The 1964 AFL Championship Game at War Memorial Stadium, a 20-7 Buffalo victory over the San Diego Chargers highlighted by Stratton's tackle heard 'round the world; the 1973 season finale when Simpson became the first running back in NFL history to surpass 2,000 yards rushing; the glorious season-opener in 1980 when the Bills ended their 20-game losing streak to hated rival Miami; the 1990 AFC Championship Game when the no-huddling Bills embarrassed the proud Raiders, 51-3, to earn their first Super Bowl berth; the heartbreaking loss to the New York Giants in that first Super Bowl, played in an emotionally-charged atmosphere as the United States had just entered the Persian Gulf War; the history-making, record-breaking comeback victory over Houston in the 1992 playoffs when Buffalo rallied from a 35-3 deficit to win in overtime, 41-38; and the head-sagging Music City Miracle defeat in the 1999 playoffs at Tennessee when the Bills were fooled in the waning seconds by the Titans' Home Run Throwback kickoff return for a touchdown.

The Sabres landed in Buffalo as a National Hockey League expansion franchise in 1970 and enjoyed almost instantaneous success. The city had long been established in the hockey world with a solid American Hockey League club nicknamed the Bisons, so when the Sabres raised the bar and brought Buffalo into the major leagues, the fans flocked to the Aud to support the team.

In just their third season the Sabres fought their way into the NHL playoffs where they extended the mighty Montreal Canadiens to six games before bowing out, and in just their fifth season, they advanced all the way to the Stanley Cup Finals before losing to the Philadelphia Flyers. It took another 24 years before the Sabres would play for Lord Stanley's coveted chalice, and again the visiting team – this time the Dallas Stars – paraded the Cup around a Buffalo ice surface as Sabres fans looked on glumly.

But the lack of a championship, frustrating as it has been, has not tarnished the legacy of this team. No, that would be left to the scandalous Rigas family. For most of their 33 seasons the Sabres have warmed our winters with their wizardry, and we have ogled the likes of Perreault, Martin, Robert, Tim Horton, Jim Schoenfeld, Danny Gare, Craig Ramsay, Phil Housley, Tom Barrasso, Mike Foligno, Alexander Mogilny, Pat LaFontaine, Michael Peca and Dominik Hasek.

There are six Sabres games contained herein: Robert's overtime goal that won Game 5 of the 1973 playoff series at the hallowed Montreal Forum; Robert's overtime goal that won Game 3 of the 1975 Stanley Cup Finals at the Aud against Philadelphia; Brad May's overtime goal in the first round of the 1993 playoffs against Boston which ended Buffalo's streak of first-round failure; Game 6 of the 1994 playoffs against New Jersey when Dave Hannan's goal in the fourth overtime ended the sixth-longest game in NHL history; Tasker's favorite moment, Plante's overtime winner in Game 7 against Ottawa in 1997 which provided HSBC Arena (then known as Marine Midland Arena) with its first noteworthy night; and Brett Hull's goal (or more aptly, "No goal") that clinched the 1999 Stanley Cup for Dallas in the third overtime of Game 6.

Basketball dominated Buffalo's sporting scene in the 1940s, 50's and 60s as Canisius, Niagara and St. Bonaventure annually churned out competitive teams. And never was the competition fiercer than when they played each other, often at the Aud in front of large and jingoistic crowds.

"It was the sport back then," said Fran Corcoran of Canisius who made one of the biggest shots in Griffs history, a basket that delivered a 79-78, four-overtime victory over heavily-favored North Carolina State in the first round of the 1956 NCAA tournament. "There was no pro basketball or pro football team, the hockey was minor league, so college basketball was the big thing. It was wonderful."

Tom Chester, a native of North Tonawanda who played for Canisius' 1963 team that lost in the finals of the NIT tournament at Madison Square Garden, concurred.

"When we played in the 50s and 60s at the Aud, it was a social event," he said. "That's one of the things you can't reproduce today, those doubleheaders at the Aud."

There were countless golden moments produced by players such as Joe Dudzick, Joe Cavanaugh, Henry Nowak, Johnny McCarthy, Bill O'Connor, Tony Masiello, Larry Fogle, Mike Smrek and Ray Hall of Canisius; Larry Costello, Alex Ellis, Ken Glenn, Al Butler, Manny Leaks, Calvin Murphy, Andy Walker, Garry Jordan and Joe Arlauckas of Niagara; and Ken Murray, Bill Butler, brothers Sam and Tom Stith, Fred Crawford, Whitey Martin, Bob Lanier, Jim Satalin, Billy Kalbaugh, Greg Sanders, Essie Hollis, Earl Belcher, Glenn Hagan, Mark Jones and J.R. Bremer of St. Bonaventure.

And Buffalo basketball was enhanced for eight years in the 1970s by the NBA Braves who were coached by, among others, Dolph Schayes and Jack Ramsay, and who trotted out such stars as McAdoo, DiGregorio, Smith, Bob Kauffman, Gar Heard, Jim McMillian, Jack Marin, John Shumate, Adrian Dantley, Billy Knight and Nate Archibald.

The six games selected for inclusion here offer representation from all these teams, plus a classic matchup at the Aud in 1971 between rivals Buffalo State and the University of Buffalo who were led, respectively, by Smith and Curtis Blackmore. There is the 1956 Canisius-North Carolina State NCAA shootout; the 1969 season finale when Canisius outlasted Niagara behind Mayor Masiello's career-best 35 points in his last game as a senior; St. Bonaventure's Final Four loss to Jacksonville when Lanier was sidelined with a knee injury; the Braves loss to the Boston Celtics in the 1974 playoffs when Jo Jo White clinched the series with a pair of free throws with no time remaining in Game 6 at the Aud; and the Braves Game 4 defeat of Washington in the 1975 playoffs when McAdoo threw in 50 points.

Finally, there is baseball, a game that has been played professionally in Buffalo – with the exception of the years 1971 – 78 – since 1877. From their days at Michigan and Ferry where old Offermann Stadium stood, to the mostly forgettable times at War Memorial Stadium, to the record-shattering attendance days at Dunn Tire Park (nee Pilot Field and North Americare Park), the Bisons have provided Buffalo with summer pleasure while earning league championships in 1915, 1916, 1933, 1936, 1957, 1961, 1997 and 1998.

Vince McNamara, the Buffalo native who once spent 37 years as president of the Class A New York-Penn League – of which one of the divisions is now named after him – grew up playing baseball on the cobblestone streets of Buffalo's First Ward in the early 1900s. He once said "Baseball is baseball, whether it's being played in Yankee Stadium or out on the sandlots."

So true.

So while Buffalo has never been "major league" in baseball, its baseball history is nonetheless rich and colorful. Buffalo has produced such major leaguers as Warren Spahn, Sal Maglie, Sibby Sisti, Buddy Rosar, Pat Dobson, Rick Manning, Joe Hesketh and Dave Hollins. And among those who have worn the uniform of the Bisons are Maglie, Hollins, Ollie Carnegie, Luke Easter, Johnny Bench, Jeff Manto, Fred Hutchinson, Lou Boudreau, Jim Bunning, Bartolo Colon, Bill Dickey, Brian Giles, Dwight Gooden, Bud Harrelson, Dallas Green, Fergie Jenkins, Cleon Jones, Ed Kranepool, Brian Giles, Steve Lyons, Lee May, Hal McRae, Joe McCarthy, Denny Neagle, Moises Alou, Tony Pena, Herb Pennock, Richie Sexson, Jim Thome, Marv Throneberry, Tim Wakefield, Vic Wertz and Don Zimmer.

Of the six games included, five were played by the Bisons, and one was the 1963 epic pitching duel between Spahn of the Milwaukee Braves and Juan Marichal of the San Francisco Giants, each of whom pitched into the 16th inning before Marichal's Giants finally prevailed. The Bisons games are Dick Marlowe's perfect game in 1952; Luke Easter becoming the first player to hit a home run over the center-field scoreboard at Offermann Stadium in 1957; Opening Day 1979 when the Bisons returned to Buffalo and Luis Salazar won the first game with a three-run homer in the bottom of the ninth; the 18-inning loss to Nashville in the one-game playoff that decided the 1990 American Association Eastern Division title; and the incredible Game 4 rally against Denver in the

AA championship series when the Bisons, down 9-0 and being no-hit through eight innings, scored eight runs in the ninth inning, only to have the tying run thrown out at the plate to end the game.

These 25 games, presented chronologically, only scratch the surface of Buffalo's sporting history, but we have to start somewhere. I hope you enjoy the stories as much as I enjoyed researching and writing them.

Sal Maiorana
August 2003

August 15, 1952 - Baltimore, Md.
Memorial Stadium

Perfection

The International League has been in business for more than 115 years, but there have been only three perfect games, and two have been authored by members of the Buffalo Bisons. Chester Carmichael did it in 1910 against New Jersey, and then in 1952 Dick Marlowe retired all 27 Baltimore Orioles he faced.

We have Bartolo Colon to thank for making the baseball-watching life of longtime Buffalo Bisons historian Joe Overfield complete.

You see, Overfield, a Buffalo treasure who passed away in July 2000 at the age of 84, spent the better part of seven decades chronicling the exploits of his favorite baseball team. It would be hard to fathom that any man, past or present, saw more Bisons games than Joe, yet in all that time, he had never witnessed a no-hitter in person.

Thankfully, Joe was up in the press box on that June evening in 1997 when Colon – the former Bisons and Cleveland Indians fireballer who now pitches for the Chicago White Sox – held the New Orleans Zephyrs hitless in a game at North Americare Park.

Colon's performance was superlative, but it wasn't the greatest pitching feat by a Bison during Overfield's lifetime. That honor belongs to Dick Marlowe, who in 1952 threw a perfect game for Buffalo against the Baltimore Orioles who were then members of the International League.

Overfield, like every other Bisons fan of that era, missed the 2-0 victory because it was played in Baltimore. And while you can bet Overfield had his ear pressed to his radio listening to Bisons announcer Bill Mazer's re-creation of the game as Marlowe set down all 27 Orioles he faced, listening to a no-hitter or perfect game on the radio and witnessing one live are two different things. Sort of like going to watch a band perform in concert, or buying their live CD.

Buffalo manager Jack Tighe – who died in 2002 at the age of 88 – said that night he was "pleasantly surprised" by Marlowe's performance given that in his previous outing, a loss to the Rochester Red Wings, his mechanics were terribly off kilter.

In that game, played on a soggy evening at War Memorial Stadium, Tighe noticed Marlowe – a lanky right-hander from Hickory, N.C. who pitched parts of six major league seasons with the Detroit Tigers between 1951 and 1956 – was slipping on a muddy spot on the mound as he was releasing the ball. During a rain delay the tarp had blown up a bit and exposed a portion of the mound to the rain, but Tighe said the muddy area should not have affected Marlowe's normal motion. However, the pitcher was striding improperly and when he kept slipping on that spot, Tighe knew something was amiss as the Red Wings lit him up.

"A pitcher's normal stride wouldn't have put him near that spot, yet Dick kept slipping on every pitch," Tighe said. "His stride was way too long so we worked on it."

Marlowe took the loss in that game against the Red Wings, and before his next start against Baltimore Tighe worked with him on his delivery. "This was the first game since and it looks like it paid off," said Tighe after Marlowe pitched what was then just the eighth perfect game in professional baseball history.

"I don't think I tensed up too much, I just kept throwing," Marlowe said. "I didn't feel any different than any other game. My fastball and my change were clicking, that's all."

Marlowe was not overpowering as he struck out just four Baltimore batters, but a mere five balls left the infield. Only two Orioles – Gerry Scala ending the eighth and Dee Phillips leading off the ninth – reached a full count on Marlowe.

"It's the first no-hitter I've caught in 13 years of pro ball, and I guess it's the first perfect game anybody has caught lately," said catcher Joe Erautt, who pointed out that Marlowe's shortened stride helped him with his control.

The Bisons scored the only runs Marlowe would need in the sixth inning when Bob Mavis hit a solo home run, then Don Lund walked, took second on Frank Carswell's single and scored on a single by Bill Tuttle.

As the innings went by, Marlowe said the magnitude of what was happening didn't really hit him. "I knew I had a no-hitter in the top of the seventh, but I didn't know until the game was over that there weren't any walks and no one got on base," he said. "When the fans started hollering at

(Courier-Express)

Jack Tighe managed the Bisons to a record of 71-83 in 1952 and 86-65 in 1953. He missed part of the 1952 season due to an emergency appendectomy, but he was in the dugout the night Dick Marlowe threw his perfect game in Baltimore. The following season, Tighe was promoted to the parent Detroit Tigers where he served as a coach.

the start of the seventh 'Go spoil your no-hitter' I just said to myself 'OK, here it goes.'"

Tighe, though, knew exactly what was happening. "I wouldn't have known except for a couple of loud fans in the stands right over the dugout," said the manager who missed part of the 1952 season due to an appendectomy. "They kept me informed."

In the ninth, Phillips popped up meekly to the infield, pinch-hitter Al Cihocki grounded out to Doc Daugherty at shortstop, and then pinch-hitter Russ Kerns tapped back to the mound and Marlowe was able to complete the perfect game by tossing Kerns out at first.

FRANK CARSWELL

When Carswell broke into professional baseball in the early 1940s fresh out of Rice University, he seemed destined to enjoy a prosperous athletic career.

He was an outstanding basketball player, one of the finest forwards to ever play at Rice, but there was no future in basketball as the NBA hadn't even been formed. But Carswell had baseball to fall back on. Blessed with blazing speed, a strong arm and a sweet hitting stroke, he was a can't-miss prospect. That is until the outbreak of World War II.

Carswell served his country as a combat captain in the Marines, and while he escaped serious injury on the European battlefields, the activity took a toll on his body. When he returned state-side and attended the Bisons' spring training in 1945, he couldn't regain his pre-war form and was cut.

He played briefly for Buffalo in 1946, then bounced around the lower minors – winning a batting title in the Big State League in 1949 with a .400 average – until he regained a position in Buffalo. And from 1951 to 1954 he was one of the best left fielders in the International League.

During the 1952 season when Carswell won the International League batting crown (.344) and home run title (30), Johnny McHale, the farm director for Buffalo's parent club, the Detroit Tigers, said "Carswell is the greatest right-hand hitter in the game and as a pinch-hitter he could decide the pennant race for either the Yankees or the Cardinals."

The Tigers opted not to trade Carswell for prospects, so he stayed in Buffalo the rest of that season and became the object of a controversy at the end of the year. Manager Jack Tighe glued Carswell to the bench the last five games, and sports writers in Rochester charged that Tighe benched Carswell to insure that he would win the IL batting crown instead of Rochester's player/manager Harry Walker.

Tighe explained that Carswell had suffered a knee injury, plus was exhausted from a long season, so with Buffalo out of the pennant race, he gave him a rest. "Carswell played a lot more games than we expected he would and he was due for a rest," said Tighe. "Harry Walker won the American Association title last year on only 298 times at bat. Well, if Walker was to win the crown this time, we felt that he should have done it the hard way."

Carswell made it to the majors briefly in 1953 with the Tigers, batting 15 times in 16 games, mostly as a pinch-hitter. Then it was back to Buffalo and he never went up again.

Those who were home in Buffalo listening on the radio didn't have to wait for the suspenseful final three outs to be recorded. In those days most teams – both in the minors and the majors – did not send their radio announcers on the road. Instead, they would sit in a studio and recreate the play-by-play of the games using a Western Union telegraph. As each at-bat would come over the wire the announcer would pretend the action was live and describe it while using sound effects such as crowd noise, the crack of the bat and the snap of a glove.

Mazer, recognizing that he was recreating a historic event, could not help but get caught up in the excitement. Like a kid sneaking down the stairs on Christmas morning, Mazer looked ahead on the telegraph machine in the ninth inning to see if Marlowe had completed the masterpiece, and when he saw that he had, he screamed into his microphone: "It's a perfect game! It's a perfect game!"

Hours after the on-field celebration, Marlowe relaxed in his Baltimore hotel room and said "I still find it hard to believe, it's just one of those things."

It took nearly 50 years for the third International League perfect game to be thrown, that by Toma Ohka of the Pawtucket Red Sox against Charlotte in June 2000, one month before Overfield died. Three perfect games in a league history that spans more than 115 years, and two of them thrown by Bisons. In his next start Marlowe gave up a two-run homer to Syracuse's Hank Workman in the first inning, but he ended up pitching a complete game and earned the victory when the Bisons rallied in the ninth to win 5-3. Eleven days after the perfect game, the Bisons held a ceremony to honor Marlowe. The team and some of its fans presented Marlowe with a bevy of gifts including an 18-inch television set, cigars, an electric clock, pants, shirts, ties, a hat, and a $100 war bond. Erautt received a fishing rod and reel for calling and catching the perfect game. Marlowe was never able to hang on for any significant period in the major leagues. He posted a record of 13-15 with an earned-run average of 4.99 with the Detroit Tigers before leaving baseball. Sadly, he was just 39 years old when he died in 1968.

March 12, 1956 – New York City
Madison Square Garden

The Basket of a Lifetime

*It was the only shot Fran Corcoran made in the game, but the Canisius senior
picked a pretty good time to score it: Three seconds left to play in the fourth
overtime of the Griffs' 1956 NCAA Tournament game at Madison Square Garden
against second-ranked North Carolina State, delivering to Canisius
one of its greatest victories.*

The picture still hangs in the Pinehurst, N.C. home of Fran Corcoran, and though it is
now 47 years old, it has held up well in the glass encased frame Corcoran placed it in so
long ago.

So, too, has the memory of what that photograph represents. It is a snapshot –
captured by a *New York Times* photographer at famed Madison Square Garden in New
York City – of Corcoran making what is still considered the biggest shot in the history
of Canisius College basketball.

It was the first round of the 1956 NCAA Tournament and the opponent was
Atlantic Coast Conference champion North Carolina State, a national powerhouse
ranked second in the country by the Associated Press behind only the Bill Russell-led
University of San Francisco. The unheralded, heavy underdog Golden Griffins pushed
the Wolfpack into a fourth overtime period, and with three seconds to go, trailing by
one, Corcoran flashed open on the right wing and let go a jumper from about 15 feet
away.

Just as the ball passed through the hoop, the *Times* photographer clicked his shut-
ter. In that split second when the flashbulb exploded, a moment in Canisius history was
preserved forever, a moment Griffs fans still cling to.

You see the ball rippling the net, and in the background you see Corcoran's eyes
lighting up while behind him, the fans at the Garden leap from their seats in excited disbelief. It was Corcoran's only basket of the game – a game that still ranks today as the
longest in NCAA tournament history – and it made the final score Canisius 79, North
Carolina State 78.

"It's funny," Corcoran said. "They say everybody has their 15 minutes of fame.
That was mine."

In the decade of the 1950s, college basketball was king in Western New York.
The NFL's Buffalo Bills did not exist. The NHL's Buffalo Sabres did not exist. The
NBA's Buffalo Braves did not exist. In terms of spectator sports, all Buffalo had was
professional minor league hockey and baseball (both teams nicknamed the Bisons), and
big-time Division I college basketball at Canisius, Niagara and St. Bonaventure, known
locally as the Little Three.

While the great rivalry between Calvin Murphy of Niagara and Bob Lanier of St. Bonaventure in the late 1960s produced more headlines and garnered more national attention, there was never a period in Little Three history that was more captivating than the 1950s when doubleheaders at the Aud were the norm, and nearly every game between the schools produced a new form of excitement.

"It was *the* sport," Corcoran says of the Little Three. "There was no pro basketball or pro football team, the hockey was minor league, so college basketball was the big thing. The doubleheaders were great. I used to love to go to the games and watch even when I wasn't playing. It was wonderful."

And led by the great Henry Nowak – who still ranks sixth on the Griffs' all-time scoring list even though he didn't have the benefit of playing four years because freshmen were ineligible in his day – Canisius ruled the roost. During Nowak's three years from 1954-55 to 1956-57, the Griffs beat their Little Three rivals 11 of 14 times, and those victories helped them secure three consecutive bids to the NCAA tournament.

(Canisius College)

Fran Corcoran made only one basket on the night of March 12, 1956, but it was the biggest one of the game and of his career. Corcoran's jump shot in the waning seconds gave Canisius a thrilling victory in the fourth overtime against North Carolina State in the NIT tournament at Madison Square Garden.

To put that achievement into perspective, in the 46 years since Nowak graduated, the Griffs have made it back to the big dance only once – in 1996 when they lost a first-round game to Utah, 72-43.

Those Canisius NCAA teams were well-honed units, coached by Joe Curran to a three-year record of 59-20, and the 1955-56 squad may have been the best in school history. Four of the Griffs' 40 all-time leading scorers – Nowak, Johnny McCarthy, Dave Markey and Greg Britz, all of whom are members of the Canisius Hall of Fame – were regulars on that team, and Corcoran, Bob Kelly, Joe Leone and Jimmy McCarthy were solid contributors during the Griffs' 17-6 regular season.

Nowak was an all-everything forward, a player who could shoot, pass, rebound and play defense. McCarthy was the point guard, a dribbling demon who in the days before the shot clock could protect leads by playing keepaway. "Nobody could take the ball from him," Corcoran said. Markey was a sweet-shooting guard, Kelly a strong rebounding forward and Leone was the center. Corcoran was the sixth man who could play guard or forward, while fellow senior Jimmy McCarthy and sophomore Britz were

---

HENRY NOWAK

It was always Nowak's way, whether he was playing basketball or playing hardball in the Congress: Speak softly, play ball, get results.

The longtime congressman remembers sitting on a barstool in a neighborhood watering hole in Black Rock drinking root beer, eating pretzels and watching Canisius College play basketball on television. He was 12, and he thought to himself "If I could get good enough, I can go there."

So he practiced and practiced at a school playground near his home, sometimes past midnight or until the cops came to shoo him home. Cut from the Riverside High team because he was too small, he sprouted to 6-foot-3 and wound up being the captain.

Just as he had dreamed, basketball was his ticket to Canisius, and no Griff ever had more of an impact than Nowak. He led Canisius to three straight appearances in the NCAA tournament between 1955 and '57 during which time the Griffs won six of nine tournament games, Nowak averaging a cool 19.4 points in those games. For perspective,

Canisius has played just one other NCAA game in the 4 1/2 decades since Nowak graduated, that in 1996.

"He was a hard-nosed player, physical," said Bob MacKinnon, who assisted head coach Joe Curran during Nowak's years at the school before later becoming head coach. "He drove to the basket, forcing the foul. He was very good at converting an ordinary play into a three-point play."

Nowak had a chance to play in the NBA for the St. Louis Hawks, but he turned it down to go to University of Buffalo law school. Upon graduation he worked in a local firm, then began his political career by surprisingly winning election as the Erie County comptroller in 1965. Soon he was off to Washington as Buffalo's Democratic representative when his predecessor, Thaddeus J. Dulski, resigned, and Nowak has been funneling federal aid to Buffalo – more than $1 billion, it is believed – ever since.

"Buffalo, to me, is the client I represent in Congress," Nowak once said.

---

also part of Curran's rotation.

Canisius started the season 2-3 and was just 11-6 after a double-overtime loss to Manhattan. But then came a six-game winning streak to close the schedule that included victories over Bowling Green, Holy Cross, Villanova, Detroit, Syracuse and Niagara, catapulting the Griffs into the 32-team NCAA field.

Their first opponent: The Wolfpack, winners of the Atlantic Coast Conference and a team many felt would be San Francisco's eventual foil in the national championship game with star 6-foot-8 center Ron Shavlik leading the way. In 1955-56 Shavlik averaged 19.5 rebounds per game and in a game against Villanova that year he had scored 49 points and grabbed 35 rebounds. When the ACC picked its 50 greatest players to celebrate the conference's 50th anniversary in 2002, Shavlik made the cut. Another star for coach Everett Case was forward Vic Molodet, who averaged 18.2 points per game and was MVP of the 1956 ACC tournament. In 2001, Molodet joined Shavlik in the North Carolina State Hall of Fame. Phil Dinardo and John Maglio were also key members of the team.

(Canisius College)

Long before Henry Nowak became a prominent congressman, he was a star for the Canisius basketball team. More than four decades after graduating, Nowak still ranks sixth on the Griffs' all-time scoring list with 1,449 points.

Although the Griffs had advanced to the Elite Eight of the NCAAs the year before, beating Williams and Villanova before losing to LaSalle, the Wolfpack showed little respect. "There was a story that went around, and I don't know if it was true, that one of the reporters in New York asked Case 'What do you think of Canisius?'" Corcoran recalled. "He said 'I'm not sure I can spell it.' Well, after the game the students sent him letters spelling it out."

From the early moments it was apparent the Griffs had not come to New York to play the role of patsy. Johnny McCarthy's set shot snapped a 6-6 tie and Canisius held the lead until Molodet drove for a basket to put North Carolina State up 30-29. Even then the Griffs came back with a 10-4 spurt to close the half ahead 39-34 as McCarthy scored 12.

Shavlik, who would finish with 25 points, really couldn't establish his usual dominance inside because the Griffs employed a collapsing zone. "Joe Leone played Shavlik in front whenever possible, and the two forwards fell off to help on Shavlik whenever they could," said Curran.

The lead ballooned to nine shortly after the intermission when Markey and Kelly each hit jumpers, and then Nowak took charge, scoring 16 of his game-high 29 points to give Canisius a 63-59 bulge with about five minutes remaining in regulation. North Carolina State surged ahead as Molodet made four free throws and Maglio swished a hook shot, but Markey nailed a corner jumper with 2:35 left to tie it at 65, and when neither team scored again, overtime dawned.

One free throw by Nowak and two by McCarthy gave Canisius a quick lead in the first extra period, but Dinardo's jumper with 20 seconds left sent the Wolfpack out front, 69-68. The Griffs went to their go-to guy Nowak, and he drew a foul with five ticks left. After making the first for the tie, he missed the second, and thus, overtime No. 2.

After Maglio and Nowak traded baskets, the Griffs gained possession, stalled until 15 seconds remained, then called timeout to set up a play for Nowak. However, his shot bounced off the rim, and at 71-71, the teams headed for the third overtime.

This one was scoreless as both teams stalled, drawing boos from the crowd of 14,522, and when each side missed the only shot it attempted, it was on to the fourth overtime. Despite fatigue beginning to set in, the teams returned to a more open style game. Leone tipped in an errant Nowak shot, but Shavlik answered with a pair of free throws. Markey and Kelly each made two from the line to put Canisius up 77-74, but Dinardo scored on a layup and Maglio stole the ball from Markey and converted a layup to put the Wolfpack in the lead at 78-77.

After the Griffs misfired on their next possession, North Carolina State grabbed the rebound and called timeout with 30 seconds to go, and upon resumption of play, Kelly fouled Maglio with 10 seconds remaining.

"What went through my mind at that point is we really put these guys through the hoops, and gosh darnit, we did the best we could," Corcoran said. "Now we're going to lose because we figured he's going to make the two foul shots."

He didn't. Maglio missed the front end of the one-and-one, Markey corralled the rebound, threw it out to McCarthy and he fed Corcoran down the right side. "All I could think was I have to get it up quick because if I miss, we can still get a rebound," said Corcoran.

No need. The ball splashed through, the Garden erupted, and when North Carolina State failed to get off a shot in the final three seconds, one of the biggest upsets in tournament history was complete.

Corcoran had played against Dinardo when the two were prepping in Philadelphia, and after the game he remembered Dinardo saying it was the worst loss he'd ever had. Same for Case. In a commemorative book about the history of ACC basketball, this game was referenced and Case was quoted as saying it was the most bitter defeat of his career.

"They really expected to be playing San Francisco in the finals," said Corcoran.

When the horn sounded, the Griffs rushed to Corcoran and hoisted him on their shoulders, giving him the ride of his life. Meanwhile, his mother missed all of the hoopla because she was too nervous to watch. "Being from Philadelphia my mom and dad never got a chance to see me play in Buffalo so they were all there," Corcoran said. "My mom is very religious and she was in the hallway, she couldn't stand to watch, so she was out there saying the rosary."

In the *New York Times* picture – which the newspaper sent to Curran, who then forwarded it to Corcoran – Markey is in the foreground, underneath the basket, prepared to play the hero's role. He laughs about it today.

"Corcoran had the ball with about three seconds to go on the clock and I was wide open under the basket," Markey said. "I can still remember taking off down the wing and being open. I could have been Corcoran's mother and he wouldn't have given me the ball. I can picture it right now, I'm under the left side of the basket and he's on the right side top. I'm wide open, nobody near me, screaming for him to give me the ball."

Corcoran's reply: "Yeah, but Markey was a terrible shooter. Jim McCarthy, who threw me the pass, went on to become a senior vice president at Merrill Lynch. I worked there, too, so he was my ultimate boss and he kidded me all the time. He'd say 'Without me, you'd never have had the opportunity.' I told him 'No way I was giving the ball up.'"

Forty-seven years have passed, and still it is the longest game in NCAA tournament history. Corcoran retired to Pinehurst, N.C. in the heart of ACC country where basketball is like religion, and every once in a while he tweaks those hoop junkies along Tobacco Road.

"When March Madness comes around there's a place down here called the Pinecrest Inn where a lot of the golfers go," Corcoran said. "I've been over there a few times and these young guys watch the games, drink beer, say they're big fans. So just for kicks I ask them if they know what the longest game ever played in NCAA history was. And they never get it. And then I say 'By the way, I'm the guy that made the winning shot.' I love it."

The Griffs took out Dartmouth in the second round in Corcoran's hometown of Philadelphia, but with a berth in the Final Four on the line, they lost a heartbreaker the next night to Temple, 60-58. Nowak, after scoring 29 points in each of the first two games, was held to nine by the Owls. So Temple joined San Francisco, Iowa and SMU in Evanston, Ill., and Russell's Dons ultimately won the title, 83-71, over Iowa. Without the graduated McCarthys, Corcoran and Kelly, the Griffs still put together a 22-6 record in 1956-57 and advanced to their third straight NCAA as Nowak – who would go on to a distinguished political career including 18 years in Congress – averaged 20.1 points. However, North Carolina knocked Canisius out in the second round, 87-75, and the Tar Heels went on to win the national championship, defeating Wilt Chamberlain and Kansas, 54-53 in three overtimes.

June 14, 1957 – Buffalo, N.Y.
Offermann Stadium

The Longest Ball

Although he played in Buffalo just over three years, and he did so when he was already past his athletic prime, no player in Buffalo Bisons history had a greater impact on the fans and was more beloved than Luke Easter. And with one swing of the bat in 1957, Easter cemented his legacy when he became the first man to hit a home run clear over the center-field scoreboard at Offermann Stadium.

Nearly half a century has passed, but Joe Altobelli still remembers the night Luke Easter of the Buffalo Bisons became the first – and only – player to hit a home run over the center-field scoreboard at old Offermann Stadium.

"In those days when you hit a ball to center field, you didn't think it was going out," Altobelli said, reminiscing about a time in baseball when center field – remember old Yankee Stadium and the Polo Grounds? – was usually a place where fly balls went to die. "Most stadiums when you hit it to center field, it was like Death Valley and it was going to be caught. Obviously, nobody caught that one."

Not unless you were on the roof of the home of Mrs. Irene Luedke, 128 Woodlawn Avenue, situated directly behind the scoreboard about 506 feet from the batters' box, which is how far the ball was estimated to have traveled. "I thought an atomic bomb hit," Mrs. Luedke exclaimed in an interview after the game. "I was all alone, sitting in the front room when I heard this terrible crash. I quick ran out to the porch and there was the ball."

The Bisons had been playing baseball on the corner of Michigan and Ferry since 1889, and Offermann Stadium had been erected on the site in 1924. In the 33 years since, no one had ever hit a ball over the 60-foot-high center-field scoreboard that stood 400 feet from home plate. There had been rumors that Babe Ruth had cleared it in batting practice prior to a 1932 exhibition game the New York Yankees played there, but Easter's was certainly the first in a regular game.

"If anybody was going to do it, it had to be him in those days," said Altobelli, who that night was playing first base for one of Buffalo's International League rivals, the Columbus Jets. "He was extraordinarily big for a baseball player in those days, about 230 pounds, and he had a hard swing. He grunted when he swung, sort of like a man wielding an axe. They used to have a right-field fence and there was a house behind it, and Luke used to hit 'em there, too. I've seen some left-handed hitters hit it a long way, but he stands out in my top three. We were both in the Cleveland organization and there were some spots in that old Municipal Stadium where he hit them that were ungodly."

One such blast in Cleveland came in a 1950 game against the Washington Senators. Easter hit what is believed to be the longest home run ever at the cavernous stadium, a 477-foot blast that sailed over the right-field upper deck auxiliary scoreboard, previously outer space for baseballs.

In 1949, Roy Campanella of the Brooklyn Dodgers overheard one of his teammates say that no one had ever hit the ball into the center-field bleachers at the Polo Grounds, 475 feet from home plate. He corrected them, pointing out that Easter did it in a 1948 Negro League game playing for the Homestead Grays against the New York Cubans. Bob Thurman, Easter's teammate, recalled the homer, saying "He hit it halfway up the stands, about 500 feet. The thing about it – it was a line drive."

Easter, the first African-American to play for Buffalo in the 20th century, was already 40 years old and on the downside of his career when the Bisons acquired him for $7,500 from Charleston (W.Va.) in 1956. His entry into the major leagues had been thwarted by the color of his skin, and it wasn't until Jackie Robinson broke down the racial barrier in Brooklyn in 1947 that Easter made it to the show with Cleveland in 1949, just the eighth black player to do so.

(Buffalo Bisons)

His career with the Bisons was a relatively short one, less than four years, but Luke Easter became one of the most beloved athletes in Buffalo sports history. Between 1956 and the early stages of 1959, Easter swatted 114 home runs.

"Luke was a jokester, easy to get along with," said Danny Carnevale, a former Indians scout who was the Bisons' general manager for a stretch in the 1950s. "He never complained or was bitter about prejudice because of the color of his skin."

It was such a shame because he was a marvelously gifted player who, had he been able to compete in his prime, might have challenged some of the sacred records of the sport, most notably Ruth's 60 home runs in a single season set in 1927.

"Had Luke come up to the big leagues as a young man, no telling what numbers he would have had," his former Cleveland teammate, Al Rosen, once said. "Instinctively, he did all the right things. Maybe there is such a thing as 'a natural.'"

Easter was 34 years old when he made it to Cleveland, and he played in the majors for parts of just six seasons because he couldn't keep his aging body from breaking down. He hit 93 major league home runs, 31 coming in 1952 when he also drove in 97 runs and was named by *The Sporting News* as its American League Player of the Year.

Demoted by the Indians in 1954, he never played in the big leagues again, instead starting a secondary minor-league career that lasted another 11 years until he was an amazing 48 years old. After a number of stops he landed in Buffalo and played at Offermann from 1956-58 plus a few weeks in 1959 before the Bisons released him and he signed with the Thruway rival Rochester Red Wings where he thrived until 1964.

PHIL CAVARRETTA

In the spring of 1954 Chicago Cubs owner William Wrigley asked his manager, Cavarretta, where he thought the ballclub might finish that season. Cavarretta, never one to mince words, gave an honest assessment. "Last," he said. So Wrigley fired him, making Cavarretta the first manager ever fired in spring training.

"Phil hated to lose and he was very honest, and that was the reason he got fired," said Hall of Famer Ralph Kiner, who played for Cavarretta's 1953 Cubs team.

Cavarretta was a Chicago icon, a native of the Windy City who had played and/or managed the Cubs for 20 years at the time of his dismissal. He played in three World Series, the first in 1935 when he was 18 years old, the second in 1938 when the Yankees dismantled the Cubs in four straight despite Cavarretta's .462 average, and the last in 1945 when he won the National League batting title and the league's MVP award.

After being fired by Wrigley, Cavarretta loped down to the South Side of Chicago and played sparingly for the White Sox for two years before finally retiring at the end of 1955 with 2,030 games to his credit and a .293 average for his career.

As a player/manager for the Cubs from 1951-53 Cavarretta's record was an uninspiring 169-213 and one of his players, Ransom Jackson, once said "In all honesty, Phil wasn't the most brilliant manager in the world." However, those Cubs teams were pitiful, and Chicago sports writer Warren Brown once opined that "Cavarretta should get a bonus for watching the Cubs every day."

Too bad Cavarretta didn't get a bonus for the all curse words he used. According to Eddie Miksis, who played for the Cubs throughout Cavarretta's managerial tenure, the manager was a legendary trash mouth. "When I was with the Cubs, we had the best swearing ballclub in the National League," Miksis said. "I'm not kidding. We had Cavarretta, Don Hoak, and Dee Fondy. There was an old couple who had box seats right behind the dugout and they couldn't take it anymore. We ran them right out of the ballpark. Every other word. It was awful."

Cavarretta proved himself as a manager when he took the Bisons job in 1956 and guided the 1957 Luke Easter-led club to the International League championship. After leaving Buffalo, he went on to coach for the Detroit Tigers, and was a minor league manager from 1965-72.

When Easter was inducted posthumously into the Greater Buffalo Sports Hall of Fame in 1997, Carnevale said "Luke Easter and Ollie Carnegie (a 1992 inductee who played in the 1920s and 30s) were the two most popular players ever in Buffalo base-ball."

Easter earned that distinction because of his prodigious home runs and an outgoing personality that was as dynamic as his swing. "He was a very optimistic guy, always had a smile on his face," said Altobelli, who later was a teammate of Easter's for three years with Rochester. "He took the time for everybody. He was always wearing a smile and he never refused to say hello to the kids or sign an autograph."

As a Bison Easter hit 114 home runs, and no doubt the most memorable was his titanic shot on this lazy, hazy June evening.

Buffalo had dropped the first game of the doubleheader with Columbus, 2-1, as Altobelli – who later gained famed as a manager when he guided the Baltimore Orioles to the 1983 World Series title – hit a solo home run in the second inning and ex-Bison Russ Sullivan lofted an RBI double in the fourth for the winning run. Buffalo's only run was driven in by Easter with a single.

In the nightcap Buffalo jumped to a 4-1 lead in the third to chase Columbus starter Roger Sawyer as Lou Ortiz belted a three-run homer and Ray Noble hit a solo shot. In the top of the fourth the Jets put together a three-run rally to tie the game, but in the bottom half, relief pitcher Steve Nagy hit a solo homer to put Buffalo back in the lead. When Columbus' Ed Burtschy walked Mike Baxes and Ortiz, the left-handed Bob Kuzava – a former World Series hero for the Yankees – was summoned to face the lefty-swinging Easter.

Kuzava's first pitch, he said, was "a darned good one, exactly where I wanted it" and Easter creamed it.

"I was guessin' that Kuzava would fastball me," said Easter. "The pitch was out there with lots on it, just where I could get it with the full wood and the full swing. I guess I was kind of mad after we lost that first game. Our bench was dead, no pep."

The bench came to life watching the ball fly majestically out of the ballpark, directly over the Pepsi bottle cap sign on the scoreboard. Buffalo manager Phil Cavarretta, a major league player for 22 years, said it was "the hardest smash I've ever seen."

Even home plate umpire Ed Sudol admitted to being stunned by the home run.

"Easter threw every ounce of his weight behind that swing," said Sudol. "It was like the perfect iron shot in golf. It began rising right away and you knew it was gone. I lost it as it crossed the sign."

Easter's home run gave the Bisons an 8-4 lead and they tacked on three more runs later in the game for an 11-4 triumph, one coming home on Easter's 400-foot double off the base of the center-field wall.

Oddly, had Easter's blast stayed in the park and hit the Pepsi bottle cap sign on the scoreboard, he would have pocketed $1,000. Ruby Pastor, owner of the Buffalo Bisons' hockey club, had offered that amount in a promotion to any player who could bang one off the bottle cap. "Too bad he missed it," Pastor said. "I really wish somebody would collect the $1,000. For going over the sign we might be able to work out some kind of a consolation prize for Luke."

Easter once told Buffalo baseball writer Cy Kritzer of his home runs, "I hit 'em and then I forget 'em." It is unlikely Easter ever forgot this one. Neither did Mrs. Luedke outside the park, nor any of the 6,488 fans who were in the park that night.

Easter finished 1957 with an IL-leading 40 home runs and 128 RBI while batting .279. Not bad for a 41-year-old, who later that year hit another ball over the center-field scoreboard. The Bisons wound up second in the league with a record of 88-66, but defeated Richmond and Miami in the playoffs to win the IL championship before losing the Little World Series to the Ralph Houk-managed Denver Bears, four games to one. After retiring from baseball in 1964, Easter returned to live in Cleveland and worked at a plant that manufactured aircraft parts. He became the chief steward for the Aircraft Workers Alliance and was in charge of more than 500 workers. Easter very often carried large sums of money around, sometimes because he would cash paychecks for his employees who could not get to the bank. Occasionally he would have a police escort, other times he would carry a small gun. On March 29, 1979, armed with the gun, Easter went to a Cleveland Trust Co. branch in Euclid, Ohio just before 9 a.m. He emerged from the bank with about $5,000 in a shopping bag. Two gunmen approached, and he was shot with a .357 Magnum at close range. After a car chase, the two – one a former plant employee – were arrested, their pockets stuffed with bank envelopes containing the workers' pay. The 63-year-old Easter died before he reached the hospital.

July 2, 1963 - San Francisco
Candlestick Park

A Pitching Duel for the Aged

Buffalo native Warren Spahn is remembered as being the winningest left-handed pitcher in Major League Baseball history, but it was a game that the Hall of Famer lost that perhaps defined his greatness. In 1963 on a chilly Bay Area night at Candlestick Park, the 42-year-old Spahn battled San Francisco's 25-year-old flame-thrower Juan Marichal for 16 incredible innings before finally losing, 1-0, on a Willie Mays home run.

It couldn't have happened in this day and age of pitch counts, set-up men, and closers fattening up their save totals and wallets by protecting a three-run lead in the ninth inning.

If any manager today pulled what Alvin Dark of the San Francisco Giants and Bobby Bragan of the Milwaukee Braves did on a chilly midsummer evening at Candlestick Park, they would probably be committed to an institution, or at the very least, be named in a grievance by players' union leader Donald Fehr.

Juan Marichal of the Giants and Buffalo's own Warren Spahn of the Braves each threw complete games which would be enough to stop the presses in these pitching-poor times. However, this game went 16 innings, and nary a reliever even stirred in the bullpen. Marichal endured the full 16 innings and the 42-year-old Spahn lasted a medically miraculous 15 1/3 before he gave up Willie Mays' solo home run in the bottom of the 16th that ended the epic, never-to-be-matched pitching duel.

"I was a little tired, but my arm wasn't stiff or sore," said Spahn, the South Park High grad who faced 55 batters, walked only one – and that was intentional – allowed nine hits, struck out two, and served up 201 pitches. "I wasn't throwing as hard at the end, but I still felt strong. You know, once you get past the ninth inning, it's sudden death. You're not looking forward at all, just taking each hitter as he comes and thinking only about the present."

Marichal, 17 years Spahn's junior, also faced 55 batters, walked four, struck out 10, gave up eight hits, and made a mind-boggling 227 pitches.

"In extra innings, you go out and say you're gonna pitch one more inning so you throw as hard as you can," said Marichal, who was five years old when Spahn began his major league career in 1942 with the Boston Braves. "I said that three or four times and kept throwing hard. I didn't get very tired."

Dark could only marvel at his young pitcher, Marichal, who more than earned his ninth consecutive victory of the season and 13th overall.

"Marichal never at any time appeared to be laboring," Dark said. "He didn't throw many breaking pitches, thus tiring his arm out. He just kept slipping across the fastball with a loose, fluid motion. He got stronger."

He also got a strong dose of inspiration from his opponent.

Dark said he considered taking Marichal out in the ninth, but the pitcher didn't want to exit, saying that if the old man on the other side could keep going, so could he.

During the first eight innings Spahn pitched a better game. In the second Orlando Cepeda singled, stole second and eventually reached third before being stranded. And in the seventh San Francisco put runners on first and second, but Spahn again wriggled out of danger.

Spahn was always a master of averting disaster. And he did it with that seemingly bionic left arm as well as a cerebrally superior approach to pitching.

"Spahn is the greatest pitcher I have ever seen, bar none," said one-time Braves pitching coach Whit Wyatt. "I have seen others who had more stuff, but none had his savvy and his knack of setting up hitters. He knows how to pitch, he pitches to weaknesses."

In the fourth Marichal got into a jam when, with two outs, Norm Larker walked and Mack Jones singled. Del Crandall then followed with a single up the middle that sent Larker scurrying home, but he never made it as Mays' throw gunned him down at the plate.

(Courier-Express)

Warren Spahn grew up in South Buffalo, attended South Park High School, and then went on to become the winningest left-handed pitcher in Major League Baseball history. His 363 victories cemented his place in the Hall of Fame.

In the top of the seventh Crandall opened with a single, but was thrown out stealing which proved critical minutes later. With two outs Spahn came up and ripped a double that almost cleared the fence in right for a home run. It would have scored Crandall, even from first, but instead the Braves came away with nothing when Marichal retired Lee Maye.

Over the final nine innings Marichal allowed only two hits, four baserunners – none of which advanced past second base – and during one stretch the powerful right - hander retired 17 men in a row.

WARREN SPAHN

On the October 1999 day when Warren Spahn and 29 other baseball immortals were honored for their selection to Major League Baseball's All-Century Team, Spahn was asked if he'd ever felt more pressure than pitching in the World Series, which he did three times.

"Well, there was the Battle of the Bulge," the Buffalo native said.

The former South Park High School star, who began his career playing first base for the junior squad of Buffalo's Lake City Athletic Club, became a war hero before he began a major league career that would result in 363 victories, the most ever by a left-handed pitcher.

Spahn became the only major-leaguer to receive a battlefield commission as he earned a Bronze Star and a Purple Heart for his bravery in Europe, and his company earned a presidential citation. Spahn's company supported the 101st Airborne Division, which turned back a two-week German counteroffensive in Belgium in late-December of 1944. The Battle of the Bulge was the decisive defeat for Hitler's Germany.

"The Germans were making a push toward England and we were surrounded," said Spahn, who was hit with shrapnel in the fight. "I remember my company didn't trust dog tags or anything, because they had our equipment and uniforms and spoke English well. One of our codes was who played second base for the Bums (the Dodgers). If a German wasn't a baseball fan, he was dead."

In a more subtle way, major league hitters were usually rendered dead when they faced Spahn.

Just before Spahn left for the war he began his big-league career for Casey Stengel's woeful Boston Braves in 1942. One day Stengel ordered Spahn to throw a brushback pitch, Spahn refused, and Stengel demoted him to the minors. "It was the worst mistake I ever made," Stengel later admitted.

Due to the war, Spahn didn't return to the Braves until 1946, and in 1947 he won 21 games, the first of 13 seasons in which he won at least 20. A 14-time All-Star and a 1973 inductee into the Baseball Hall of Fame, Spahn made it look easy, made it look fun because, after all, it was just baseball.

"After what I went through overseas, I never thought of anything I was told to do in baseball as hard work," he said. "You get over feeling like that when you spend days on end sleeping in frozen tank tracks in enemy threatened territory. The Army taught me something about challenges and about what's important and what isn't. Everything I tackle in baseball and in life I take as a challenge rather than work."

Spahn moved to Oklahoma after he made it to the majors, but he never forgot his roots. "I'm so grateful," he said of his life in baseball. "Here's a guy from Buffalo, New York, who managed to play in the big leagues and earn a living at it, even though I only earned $80 a month my first year. But other guys were earning $65 out of high school, going into the steel mills."

The game appeared to end in dramatic fashion in the bottom of the ninth when Willie McCovey sent a Spahn pitch soaring over the right field foul pole. To most observers the ball was fair, but umpire Chris Pelekoudas waived it foul, so the game wore on.

"Larry Jansen, who was right on the line, said it was at least four feet fair," an angry Dark said.

"The way to avoid that is to spend a little money and build a taller foul marker," Bragan said. "In Los Angeles there wouldn't have been any question whether it was fair or foul. If they had a marker like that here, the game might have ended seven innings sooner."

In the 14th the Giants threatened to win it, but Spahn reached into his bag of tricks and again came out unscathed. Harvey Kuenn blooped a double into short center to open the inning, then Spahn walked Mays intentionally, ending a streak of 31 1/3 innings without allowing a free pass.

Spahn set down McCovey and Felipe Alou, but when third baseman Dennis Menke booted Cepeda's ground ball, the bases were loaded. Bragan stayed in the dugout and let Spahn continue, and he was rewarded when Spahn induced Ed Bailey to line out to center.

(Courier-Express)

Before Warren Spahn went on to major league greatness, he played for South Park High School. This shot was taken circa 1937. Spahn is in the back row, sixth from the left.

In the bottom of the 16th Kuenn led off by flying out, but Mays – a meek 0-for-5 – took a mighty cut at Spahn's next delivery and sent the ball soaring through the now bitterly chilly night and far over the left field fence for the game-winning homer.

"I creamed it," Mays said.

"He hit a screwball that hung," Spahn said. "It didn't break at all. What makes me mad is that I had just gotten through throwing some real good ones to Kuenn. But this one ... "

Sitting in the press box watching the game was Carl Hubbell, the former great Giants pitcher who at this time was head of the Giants' farm system. Thirty years earlier to the day Hubbell had thrown an 18-inning complete game shutout victory for the Giants, winning 1-0 over the Cardinals in the longest 1-0 game ever. But Hubbell was in his prime, while Spahn was far past his.

"He ought to will his body to medical science," Hubbell said of Spahn. "The world should be told what that man is made of and how it all got together like it did. Here is a guy, 42 years old, who still has a fastball. He just kept busting them in on the hands of our guys and kept getting them out. My arm was tired and the fastball was gone and I was through at 40. Spahnie's got me by two years and he's still throwing 15-inning shutouts."

Walker Cooper, Spahn's teammate and catcher for four seasons (1950-53), once called Spahn "a lousy 20-game winner." Spahn said when he heard that, "I made up my mind I was going to become a good 20-game winner." He became so good at it, he won 20 games in a season 13 times, the last in 1963 when he won 23. When his fabulous career ended in 1965, Spahn had a record of 363-245, still the winningest left-hander of all time. He pitched in 750 games for 5,246 innings, starting 665 and completing 382 with 63 shutouts. Marichal led the league in victories (25) and innings pitched (321) in '63 and helped San Francisco to a third-place finish, 11 games behind the eventual World Series champion Dodgers. Marichal played 16 years, retiring in 1975 with a record of 243-142 and an ERA of 2.89. He started 457 games, completed 244 with 52 shutouts, and like Spahn, is a member of the Hall of Fame.

December 26, 1964 – Buffalo, N.Y.
War Memorial Stadium

The Tackle Heard 'Round the World

During the 43-year history of the Buffalo Bills there have been countless great plays made by countless great players, but one stands alone and has withstood the test of time: Mike Stratton's crushing tackle of San Diego's Keith Lincoln that altered the course of the 1964 AFL Championship Game and ultimately keyed Buffalo's victory.

At the time, it was just another tackle, one that effectively disrupted a routine play early in a big game.

But in the minutes that Keith Lincoln lay painfully prone on the frozen War Memorial Stadium muck, clutching his broken ribs after Mike Stratton had driven him ruthlessly into the ground, a Buffalo legend was born.

"That was one of the most beautiful tackles I have ever seen in my life," conceded San Diego coach Sid Gillman. "That is the name of the game."

Stratton's textbook shoulder-to-midsection wallop of Lincoln was the play that turned the 1964 AFL Championship game irreversibly in Buffalo's favor as the Bills used that emotional springboard to roll to a 20-7 victory, thus delivering to the city it's first pro football championship.

Stratton's hit quickly became known around Western New York as "The Tackle Heard 'Round the World" and longtime observers of the Bills who were there that cold December day or saw it on television still call it the play that changed the course of Buffalo's football history. Nearly 40 years have passed, and "The Tackle" continues to live in infamy, a moment forever etched into Buffalo sports lore.

"You could just see the emotions and the credibility of the Buffalo Bills come together at that point," said Jack Kemp, quarterback of that Buffalo team. "That hit and that win put Buffalo on the major league sports map."

Pro football had existed in Buffalo during the late 1940s when the city had a team in the old All-America Football Conference. But when that ill-fated league folded following the 1949 season, the Buffalo team was disbanded, and it wasn't until the birth of the American Football League in 1960 that Western New Yorkers would be able to follow their own pro team again.

Detroit businessman Ralph Wilson was granted an expansion club – for the whopping price of $25,000 – and his original intention was to play in Miami. When that deal fell through, he nearly gave up on his dream of becoming the owner of a pro football team.

That's when Dallas oil tycoon Lamar Hunt, who had started this whole AFL revolution, intervened. Desperate for franchise owners, Hunt called Wilson and told him five cities were hot for football – Buffalo, Louisville, Cincinnati, St. Louis and Atlanta – and Hunt would approve whichever city Wilson chose.

Wilson had connections to none of those places, so he consulted a pair of Detroit business colleagues. "I said to both of them, 'Even if you were goofy enough to go into a new speculative pro football league and buck the established NFL, which of these five cities would you pick?'" Wilson recalled. "They both said Buffalo and when I asked why, they said that Buffalo had good attendance in the All-America Conference, it was a good football city, an industrial city similar to Detroit on a smaller scale. And Buffalo had been without football for 10 years and wanted it back, so that was their choice."

Wilson surely must have wondered what he had gotten himself into. War Memorial Stadium was barely functional, the city was lukewarm to the team, and under coach Buster Ramsey the Bills won just 12 of 28 games their first two years. Wilson had said he would give it three years before re-evaluating his stake, so he fired Ramsey, hired Lou Saban, and waited to see what Saban would do in 1962.

The Bills lost their first five games that year and their future in Buffalo was tenuous at best. But they lost just one of their last nine, so Wilson stayed put, and in 1963 the team tied for first place in the AFL's Eastern Division with the Boston Patriots.

Although Buffalo blew an opportunity to play the Chargers for the AFL Championship when they lost the special playoff game at home to the Patriots, it was obvious they were a team on the rise, and in 1964, they rose above everyone else.

The Bills won their first nine games and ultimately ran away with the East, posting a 12-2 record, earning them the right to host the AFL Championship Game against Gillman's Chargers who had finished first in the West for the fourth time in five years.

The storyline was obvious: Buffalo's stout defense led by Stratton, Tom Sestak, Ron McDole, and George Saimes, against San Diego's high-octane offense that would surely miss injured star receiver Lance Alworth, but still featured quarterback Tobin Rote and backs Lincoln and Paul Lowe.

Less than four minutes into the game, San Diego was in the lead. Lincoln broke a 38-yard run on the first play from scrimmage, and three snaps later, the 38-year-old Rote – who would announce his retirement after the game – fired a 26-yard touchdown pass to Dave Kocourek.

Buffalo punted on its first possession, and the Chargers were on the move again when Stratton altered the course of the game.

(Robert L. Smith)

Buffalo linebacker Mike Stratton executed this textbook tackle on San Diego's Keith Lincoln in the first quarter of the 1964 AFL Championship Game at War Memorial Stadium. Lincoln was knocked out of the game and the Bills went on to a 20-7 victory.

Rote lobbed a swing pass into the left flat to Lincoln, and just as Lincoln reached up to catch the ball, Stratton drove his right shoulder into the running back's rib cage, wrapped him up with both arms and slammed him to the ground. The ball fell incomplete, and like three of Lincoln's ribs, the Chargers were cracked.

"You can always tell when you get a good lick, I just didn't know it would have that kind of effect," said Stratton. "When I got up I just figured Keith would get up, we'd go back to the huddle and we'd start over again on the next play. When he didn't go back

BILLY SHAW

It shouldn't have taken as long as it did, the induction of the first player into the Pro Football Hall of Fame who played his entire career in the American Football League, but at least the selectors chose the right man to break the barrier.

"Waiting 30 years for this makes it very, very special," said Shaw just prior to the August 1999 afternoon when his bronze bust was put on permanent display in the Canton, Ohio shrine. "And to represent all of the guys that toiled in the AFL in obscurity for those many years makes it all much more special."

Shaw played nine years with the Bills (1961-69), coming to the team as a second-round pick in 1961. He was an all-AFL first-team choice six times and as Bobby Bell, the Kansas City Chiefs linebacker who also is enshrined in the Hall of Fame, once said "When you had a game against the Bills, you had to bring your lunch because Billy would battle you for the entire game."

Shaw's skill was unmatched, his technique was perfect, his composure never wavered, and in the defining game of his career, the most important game he ever played as a Bill – the 1964 AFL championship – all three of those attributes melded together in symphonic harmony.

Shaw's primary foil that day was Ernie Ladd, the mountainous star defensive tackle of the Chargers. Ladd was every bit as feared in the AFL as Deacon Jones in the NFL, a 6-foot-9, 290-pound quarterback-devouring, running back-swallowing machine.

"Ernie Ladd brought tears to my eyes," said former Bills defensive end Tom Day, who played offensive guard briefly when he joined the team in 1961. However, before the game, Ladd fumbled away any physical advantage he may have had over Shaw.

"When they introduced the San Diego players, Ladd ran out between the goal posts, then pointed across the field at me," Shaw remembered. "That's what got me ready."

Ladd had seven inches and 40 pounds on Shaw, but by the time Buffalo's 20-7 victory was complete, the Big Cat had been reduced to a little kitten. The Bills rushed for 219 yards, including 122 by Cookie Gilchrist, most of them following in the cleat marks Shaw had implanted on Ladd's body.

"Of all the offensive linemen I played with in my 10 years, other than Ron Mix (also a Hall of Famer), my old roommate with the Chargers, Billy Shaw is the greatest lineman in the history of the American Football League," said ex-Bills quarterback Jack Kemp. "He ranked right there, parallel with Mix."

to the huddle, truthfully, I was happy. I didn't want him to be hurt badly, but good gosh, he'd already wreaked havoc on us before, and not to have him play certainly enhanced our chances of winning."

Stratton explained the genesis of the play this way: "It's a play that was commonly run, a flare by the back out of the backfield. The split end would run a curl 10-12 yards downfield and the key would be on the linebacker in a man-to-man defense. If the linebacker came up, (Rote) could hit the curl. If the linebacker went back to help against the curl, you dump it off to the back. It was a win-win for the offense."

Not on this day. Not on this play.

"I keyed on Rote and I could see he was looking for a receiver downfield and couldn't find one," said Stratton. "As soon as I saw that, I sprinted for Lincoln. One second earlier and it's pass interference and one second later it's a missed tackle. He rolled over and I heard him groan. I thought he had the wind knocked out of him, but then he didn't get up. I knew he was really hurt."

Lincoln, who ironically would become a teammate of Stratton's with Buffalo in 1967, did not harbor any ill will toward Stratton.

"A couple years later, Keith joined us with Buffalo and he and I became good friends," said Billy Shaw, Buffalo's Hall of Fame offensive guard. "We talked about that hit often, and he said he'd never been hit harder either before or after. Mike Stratton was a great linebacker for us."

From the moment Lincoln was helped off the field, the Chargers offense became stagnant. Already without Alworth, now they would have to make do without Lincoln, and minus his two primary weapons, Rote couldn't sustain any ball control and the talented Bills defense dominated the rest of the day.

Meanwhile, the Chargers had no answer for Buffalo running back Cookie Gilchrist. So much talk had been centered on San Diego's Lincoln/Lowe duo that Gilchrist had somehow gotten lost in the shuffle even though he led the AFL with 981 rushing yards in 1964.

Forty years since retiring from the NFL at the peak of his career, Jim Brown's legacy has withstood the test of time and in many circles he is still considered the greatest running back in league history. Funny, but former Bills cornerback Butch Byrd will make the argument that Brown wasn't even the

(Robert L. Smith)

Billy Shaw was one of the greatest offensive linemen to ever play the game, a fact that was confirmed in 1999 when he was elected to the Pro Football Hall of Fame.

best running back of his era. Byrd's vote would go to his old Buffalo teammate, Gilchrist.

"Jim Brown was the great back during that era, but I have often said that I thought Cookie was every bit as good as Jim Brown," Byrd said. "The Buffalo Bills weren't the team that the Cleveland Browns were at that time, but taking nothing away from Jim Brown, man for man, talent for talent, Cookie was right there."

Gilchrist was an unbelievably gifted athlete, a large, powerful man who could run, catch, block and tackle if he had to. He even kicked extra points and field goals. "He was probably the best athlete that I have ever played ball with," said Shaw. "He had tremendous strength and he was exceptionally quick for a man who weighed 250 pounds."

But for as talented as Gilchrist was, he was every bit as enigmatic, a dynamic personality who often clashed with leadership. Ultimately, it was that character flaw that prompted Saban to trade Gilchrist – despite his greatness – to Denver after the '64 championship game.

"He could be an All-Pro today," said Bills' owner Ralph Wilson. "He and Bronko Nagurski of the Bears were probably the two best fullbacks I ever saw."

Gilchrist gained 122 of Buffalo's 219 rushing yards against the Chargers and his running helped set up a pair of short Pete Gogolak field goals as well as fullback Wray Carlton's four-yard TD plunge that gave Buffalo a 13-7 lead, and it stayed that way heading into halftime when Stratton stopped a potential San Diego scoring drive at the Bills 15 with an interception. The only score of the final 30 minutes turned out to be Kemp's one-yard sneak with 9:12 left to play in the fourth quarter after he had thrown a 51-yard pass to Glenn Bass.

"Our defense played good, but we just didn't score," said Rote. "I really thought we had these guys. The way we started, I thought I could do the job. But then Lincoln got hurt and he's a hell of a player."

Stratton's tackle is what he is remembered most for, but that one play isn't why he is enshrined on the Bills' Wall of Fame. During his 11 years in Buffalo Stratton was the consummate pro, and he played well in good times and in bad. A 13th-round draft choice in 1962 out of Tennessee, he played in the AFL All-Star Game six times and finished his career with 21 interceptions, 18 as a Bill. "I enjoyed all my time in Buffalo," he said. "When I went up there as a rookie, being from the south I didn't know what to expect. I found out they were the nicest folks and gave us the best support that any team could ask for and they have proven that every year." The Bills would go on to repeat as AFL champions in 1965, again defeating the Chargers, this time out in San Diego by an even more dominating 23-0 count. In 1966 the Bills fell short in their quest for a three-peat, losing 31-7 in the AFL title game to Kansas City and therefore missing an opportunity to play in the first Super Bowl opposite NFL champion Green Bay. Thereafter, hard times befell Wilson's team, and it wasn't until 1974 – after the AFL had merged with the NFL and Stratton had retired – that the Bills would play another postseason game.

March 8, 1969 – Buffalo, N.Y.
Memorial Auditorium

Mayor's Ball

The battles that confront Buffalo Mayor Tony Masiello today are far greater than those he fought as the star member of the Canisius College basketball team in the late 1960s. Then again, those Little Three skirmishes with Niagara and St. Bonaventure sure were special, none better than Masiello's final game in 1969 when he scored a career-high 35 points and outplayed Purple Eagles' All-American and future Basketball Hall of Famer Calvin Murphy to lead the Griffs to an emotional victory.

Mayor Tony Masiello still gets teased about it to this day, sometimes right in his office at City Hall, about how he never passed up an opportunity to shoot the basketball during his esteemed three-year career at Canisius College.

And Masiello doesn't deny that he was a first-rate gunner because it's the truth. You could look it up. More than three decades after his transformation from star athlete to noted politician, he still ranks 18th on the school's all-time scoring list with 1,069 points because during his era he was the Golden Griffins' best player, and when coach Bob MacKinnon needed points, he turned to the kid they called Tony The Red.

But in the game that ultimately cemented Masiello's legacy in Buffalo sports lore, a pulsating 83-79 victory over Little Three rival Niagara and its superstar, Calvin Murphy, it was a shot he didn't take that provides him his most vivid remembrance of that night at Memorial Auditorium.

"My junior and senior years we didn't have too many scorers," Masiello explained. "So the game started and we were losing something like 20-6 (actually 29-15), and coach MacKinnon called a timeout after I had thrown the ball away on a pass. He grabbed me by the back of my jersey and said 'You're out there to shoot, not to pass.'"

Ever obedient, Masiello proceeded to score a career-high 35 points including the go-ahead free throws with 15 seconds remaining, and the two clinching freebies with one tick to go, touching off a raucous celebration.

So overwhelmed by what he had just witnessed, MacKinnon called it "as great a Little Three performance by an individual as I've seen." So overwhelmed were his team-mates that some of them broke down in tears as they carried Masiello into the locker room. And so overwhelmed was Masiello by what he had accomplished, he can still recall the ecstasy that enveloped he and the Griffs.

"It was an emotional night because it was the last game for many of us, four or five of us who came in together, and our careers were ending on an upbeat note," said Masiello, who began fine-tuning his smooth stroke by shooting at a basket that was nailed to a tree in the backyard of his home on the West side of Buffalo. "We were a close-knit team, we had a losing season, so beating Calvin and Niagara made it a very emotional evening."

The rivalry between Canisius and Niagara continues to simmer, but in Masiello's day the twice-a-year get-togethers between the two schools boiled over with excitement, and the vivaciousness of the competition created a frenetic atmosphere that often shook the foundation of the rickety old pre-refurbished Aud. "That place was electric during those days," Masiello remembered.

The 1968-69 basketball season had been a grossly disappointing one in Western New York. Bob Lanier and his St. Bonaventure Bonnies had been placed on a one-year NCAA probation for a minor recruiting violation and were deemed ineligible for post-season play, so their 17-7 record went for naught. Meanwhile, by the time the calendar flipped from 1968 to 1969 Canisius and Niagara had scuttled thoughts of reaching the NCAA or NIT tournaments. The Griffs were 6-16 and Niagara – despite the scoring wizardry of Murphy – were 11-12 when they took the Aud floor for this season finale. So nothing except Buffalo bragging rights were on the line, but that was usually enough to stir the embers for these two teams. "It was a phenomenal rivalry," Masiello said.

During his three years on Main Street Masiello had tasted victory over Niagara in three of five games including a 70-60 decision a couple months earlier. With about five minutes left in the first half, it looked very much like Masiello

(Canisius College)

Before he became the Mayor of Buffalo, Tony Masiello was the star player for the Canisius basketball team between 1967-69. Twice he led the Griffs in scoring average and he wound up with 1,069 points in his career.

would be settling for a career split as the Eagles raced to a 14-point lead. But after MacKinnon tongue-lashed Masiello, the senior responded with a couple baskets to key an 11-1 surge, and then Gene Roberson's two baskets pulled the Griffs within 38-37 at the half.

According to Purple Eagles coach Frank Layden, one of the keys to Canisius' rally was the foul trouble encountered by Niagara forward Steve Schafer. When Schafer had to sit, Layden assigned center Bob Churchwell to guard Masiello, and with Churchwell away from his comfort zone in the lane, Masiello lit him up from the outside.

"That's when Masiello started to go," said Layden. "He took Churchwell to the outside away from the boards and that gave them the boards. Until Schafer ran into foul trouble, we had Masiello. But with Schafer out of the game, it was a mismatch."

Schafer played only briefly in the second half, and when he was on the floor, being on the brink of disqualification sapped him of his aggressiveness and Masiello preyed on that weakness. Masiello had 13 points at the break, but went for 22 in the second half including a pivotal stretch when he scored four consecutive baskets to turn a 60-57 Canisius deficit into a 65-60 lead.

Meanwhile, Murphy was enduring a frustrating night. The Griffs had employed a stout zone defense in their previous victory over Niagara and they had held Murphy to a meager 16 points that night. Though Murphy finished with 25 in this game, his difficulties continued. The Griffs stayed in the zone, prevented Murphy from driving to the basket, and the 5-foot-10 All-American who was the third-leading scorer in the country wound up making just 10 of 30 shots from the field.

"We had preached all week that we'd zone," said MacKinnon. "We were going to stay in zone even if we fell back by 20. We weren't going to switch."

One of the most dynamic athletes to ply his craft in Buffalo, Calvin Murphy was a scoring wzard for Niagara University in the late 1960s and early 1970s. He is the school's all-time leading scorer with 2,548 points.

Led by Murphy and Churchwell (who also had 25 points plus 12 rebounds) Niagara fought back, and in the closing minutes neither team led by more than a deuce. Canisius' Roger Brown made a steal and converted a lay-up to give the Griffs a 77-75 lead with 2:30 left, and after Churchwell made a free throw, Canisius regained possession with less than two minutes to go and tried to run out the clock. The Griffs whittled away more than a minute, but Murphy foiled the plan when he stole a pass and fed Churchwell for a layup that put Niagara ahead 78-77.

Canisius regained the lead when Roberson sank a pair of free throws, and then a critical moment occurred with 36 seconds to go. Just before Murphy let go a shot that swished through the net, a foul was called on Roberson and the basket was waved off as the Niagara supporters screamed in disbelief. Then again, with Murphy going to the free-throw line to shoot one plus the bonus, there wasn't too much to worry about. Murphy was a superb free throw shooter – he once held the NBA record for most consecutive free throws made at 78 – and making a pair in this situation was almost a given. However, after sinking the first to tie the game at 79-79 he missed the second, and now it was the Canisius fans screaming in disbelief.

CALVIN MURPHY

Although he had averaged 33.1 points per game in his dazzling three-year varsity career at Niagara, there were skeptics throughout the NBA who doubted whether the diminutive 5-foot-9 Murphy would have an impact in the league of the giants.

The management of the expansion Buffalo Braves were among the doubters. They could have drafted the 1970 consensus first-team All-American with their inaugural pick, but they chose Princeton forward John Hummer instead, and Murphy slipped to the first pick of the second round, taken by the San Diego Rockets who moved to Houston the next year.

"Alex Hannum, my rookie coach, told me, 'Murph, you've got a lot of weight on your shoulders – not just for yourself. People are looking to see what you do before they start giving other little guys a chance,'" Murphy said. "I didn't have the luxury of coming in and waiting my turn. I had to make an impact quickly, not just for myself but for the little guy."

What an impact he made. Murphy scored 17,949 points, an average of 17.9 per game, he holds the NBA record for highest free-throw percentage in one season (.958 when he made 206 of 215 in 1980-81), and for more than a decade he held the record of 78 straight free throws made.

All that on the heels of his never-to-be-duplicated career at Niagara. He averaged 49 points per game for the Purple Eagles' freshman team in 1966-67, then went on to score 2,548 varsity points which ranks him No. 1 all-time in school history. In one 1968 game against Syracuse, he went for 68.

"If there had been a three-point line back then, he would have scored 100," Dr. Al Bax, Niagara's long-time team doctor, said of that game.

Murphy played his entire 13-year career with the Rockets franchise, retiring in 1983, and he was elected to the Basketball Hall of Fame in 1993.

"So much of my career was that I wasn't supposed to do things," Murphy said upon learning of his induction. "Me setting a couple of records had a lot to do with people doubting me. And I spent a lot of time trying to prove these so-called experts wrong. To beat those odds all the time and to be considered for the Hall of Fame is in itself an honor.

"I've come a long, long way in my basketball career from the first day I took a jump shot. People talk about, `What if you were 6-3 or 6-4?' Well I might not have had the motivation that I had being 5-9. This was a lot of hard work and sacrifice over the years."

Following a timeout, the Griffs moved the ball up court and to no one's surprise it ended up in Masiello's hands. The senior remembered what MacKinnon had told him – "You're out there to shoot, not to pass" – so he drove to the basket and drew a foul by Schafer with 15 seconds left, ending Schafer's night. Masiello stepped to the line panting in exhaustion – "I was getting a little tired near the end" – but he summoned enough energy to calmly make both free throws for an 81-79 lead.

Naturally, Niagara looked to Murphy for an answer, but his jump shot clanged off the rim, and when possession of the rebound could not be attained by either side, a jump ball was called with six seconds left. Roberson out-jumped Churchwell, Masiello retrieved the ball, and Churchwell was forced to foul him just before the clock ran out. Masiello again made both to clinch the victory, and one second later hundreds of Canisius fans spilled onto the court, cheering uncontrollably as Masiello was hoisted onto the shoulders of his teammates for an unforgettable ride.

"It was really a back and forth, nip and tuck game, an exciting experience," Masiello said. "Layden said many years later that was one of the best basketball games he ever coached in. It was an in-your-face game, lots of shooting and scoring, a tense and exciting evening, and when it was over the fans came onto the floor."

When the Griffs reached the locker room, Brown and Roberson jumped onto a trainers' table and shouted "We won it for Tony, the greatest leader ever."

And then more cheers, and more tears.

"Tony, (Tom) Pasternak and the others were so overwhelmed, they just had to let it go," said MacKinnon. "The tears came, and I guess they came to all of us. Considering all that we've been through, it was a great finish."

Masiello will never forget it, and he admitted that even more than the game itself, what he misses most from his days at Canisius are the bonds he formed with his teammates.

"There was a lot of hugging, a lot of expression of deep genuine support for one another," he said. "What I miss most is the camaraderie of the guys in the locker room. The guys hanging out together, celebrating together."

Masiello was drafted by the Indiana Pacers of the ABA, and though he was cut from the squad, he said he used the bonus money he received to buy a stove and refrigerator. He later tried out for the Buffalo Braves when the city was awarded an NBA franchise, but again, Masiello didn't make it. With basketball at a dead end, he turned to politics. In 1971 he was elected to the first of three terms as North District Common Council member, and he was elected to the State Senate in 1980 and won re-election five times. In 1993, he became Mayor of Buffalo and is currently in the midst of his third term.

March 19, 1970 - College Park, Md.
Cole Field House

Wounded Knee

It was the saddest of times for the St. Bonaventure basketball program in
March 2003 when the school was rocked by a player eligibility scandal that made
embarrassing national headlines. However, shedding tears is nothing new for
Bonnie fans who cried an ocean's worth back in 1970 when their team's magical
run to the Final Four was curtailed and their dreams of a national championship
shattered by Bob Lanier's knee injury.

What if?

Those two words have haunted St. Bonaventure University for 33 years, and
given the likelihood that the Bonnies will never win college basketball's national championship, they will eternally haunt the tiny Franciscan school in Olean that once dared to
dream of hoop heaven.

In Western New York sporting parlance, "What if?" is the basketball equivalent to
football's "Wide right" and hockey's "No goal." Dastardly two-word phrases that boil the
blood of the region's championship-starved fans.

What if All-American center Bob Lanier hadn't torn up his knee in the 1970
NCAA East Regional Final against Villanova, a game the Bonnies won, 97-74, to
advance to the Final Four?

What if Lanier – the best college player in the land that year, the first pick of the
1970 NBA Draft a few months later by the Detroit Pistons, and a man who would ultimately earn induction into the Pro Basketball Hall of Fame – had been able to play
when upstart St. Bona met Jacksonville in the national semifinals?

Would the Bonnies have won that game, and would they have then beaten John
Wooden's perennial powerhouse UCLA team in the national championship game at Cole
Field House on the campus of the University of Maryland?

Without reservation, Billy Kalbaugh, the co-captain of that St. Bona team along
with Lanier, said, "We'd have won. At the time he went down we were playing as well
as anybody. On any given night we could have beaten anybody, and that includes
UCLA."

To which then-St. Bona coach Larry Weise agreed. "I have no question we would
have won."

Perhaps they would have. Remember, while that UCLA team was superb, it was a
team in transition. Lew Alcindor had graduated, and Bill Walton would not begin playing until the following year. With unheralded Steve Patterson at center, the Bruins lost
twice during the regular season, and when the tournament started, they were ranked No.
2 behind Kentucky. Three starters – Henry Bibby, Curtis Rowe and Sidney Wicks –

went on to decent NBA careers, but Weise will forever be convinced that his gutsy team, with   its big-man superstar, would have handled UCLA.

"Bob was unstoppable," Weise said. "If they'd have doubled up on him, the rest of our team was balanced and could score and he was good at getting the ball out to them if they were open. My guards (Kalbaugh and Paul Hoffman) wouldn't have been outplayed. Plus, going in, I think we would have had the energy level to carry us."

But we'll never know because fate cruelly conspired against the Bonnies during the madness of that March. When Villanova's Chris Ford – who would go on to join Lanier in the NBA and later become coach of the Boston Celtics – accidentally crashed into big Bob's right knee, time ran out on this once-in-a-lifetime team, their golden moment ripped just like Lanier's medial collateral ligament.

It was such a shame. And for the Bonnies of that era, the Bonnies of every era since, and the Bonnies of eras to come, the question will always reverberate throughout the Allegheny mountains that surround the campus: What if?

The story begins at the Masten Boys Club gymnasium on Masten Street on the East side of Buffalo, circa 1961, where a 13-year-old boy learned how to play basketball. Despite being bigger than the rest of the kids his age, when Lanier first happened upon the Boys Club he wasn't interested in basketball, preferring to play baseball and, believe it or not, ping pong. But then he met the physical education director, Lorrie Alexander, and the man whose gruff exterior masked a tender, caring heart, altered the course of Lanier's life.

"I'd hate to think what would have happened if it hadn't been for Mr. Alexander," Lanier said. "He got me started in basketball. Oh, how that man worked me. Run, run, run. And the rope – the jump rope. I'll never forget it. He'd have me working with it all the time."

That's because Lanier was awkward athletically, and Alexander literally had to teach him how to run without falling

(St. Bonaventure University)

In the spring of 1970 it looked like St. Bonaventure was destined to do the unthinkable – win the NCAA basketball championship. However, when Buffalo native and Bennett High grad Bob Lanier was felled by a knee injury in the regional final, the Bonnies hopes were crushed.

down. It was a laborious process. Lanier tried out for the Bennett High varsity team as a sophomore and was cut, not only for his lack of coordination but for his lack of toughness. He was a big 'ol softy, and by refusing to use his size to his advantage, the other boys would push him around under the basket.

Alexander continued to drill the fundamentals, but one day he read the riot act to Lanier, telling him that if he didn't toughen up, he was never going to make it. Lanier paid heed, and there was no stopping him.

Although his two-year high school career was largely unspectacular, it was hard for college scouts to ignore his 6-foot-10 body, so he did attract attention from various schools around the country. However, he made up his mind that he wanted to remain in Western New York so his parents could watch him play, and he ultimately chose St. Bonaventure over Canisius.

Weise – who had replaced legendary Eddie Donovan as the Bonnies' coach five years earlier when Donovan left to become coach of the NBA's New York Knicks – knew Lanier was special the first time he saw him play. "Three things stood out in my mind," he recalled. "First, of course, was the size and the way he moved so well. Second, the great touch around the basket, the good hands. Finally, the fact that he passed off a lot which indicated to me that he was a team-type player."

Waiting for Lanier to complete his freshman year of school so he could become eligible for the varsity was certainly the longest 12 months of Weise's life. But the wait was worth it.

In Lanier's sophomore year the Bonnies won their first 23 games before losing to Dean Smith and North Carolina in the NCAA tournament, then losing a meaningless tournament consolation game to Columbia. The next year, Weise was informed by the NCAA just before the start of practice in October that the school was being hit with a minor recruiting violation, rendering it ineligible for post-season play. With nothing but pride to play for – there was no quit in these Bonnies – Weise's team still went 17-7, swept all four games against its Little Three rivals Niagara and Canisius, and set its sights on the big prize in 1969-70.

When the Bonnies convened for their first practice in October 1969, they were greeted by a chalkboard message that read: "College Park, Md." That was the site of the Final Four, and that's where the bar was set. Nothing less would do for this team.

"We had been through so much for the two years before that," Lanier said. "We knew what we wanted to accomplish, but more important, we understood what we had to do to get there and we were willing to do that."

Lanier was the hub, surrounded by Kalbaugh and Hoffman at guard and Greg Gary and sophomore newcomer Matt Gantt at forward. On the bench there was Mike Kull, Dale Tepas, Gene Fahey, Vic Thomas and Tom Baldwin. This was a solid team, regardless of one pre-season magazine's assertion that "The Bonnies are very, very ordinary."

The season began with a 106-54 wipeout of Detroit College, and after one-sided wins over Xavier, Detroit, Duquesne and New York University, the Bonnies traveled to Madison Square Garden for the prestigious Holiday Classic, their first real test of the year. They whipped St. Joseph's in the first round, setting up a match with Big Ten favorite Purdue. It was no match at all. Lanier exploded for 50 points in a 91-75 victory, and when the next AP poll was released, the Bonnies were No. 5.

St. Bona won its first 12 games before stumbling at Villanova, 64-62, and then it trailed rival Niagara and Calvin Murphy by 11 in the second half at home in its next outing before rallying for an 89-81 victory that righted the ship.

From there the Bonnies closed the regular season with nine wins, the closest of which was a 10-point defeat of Long Island, and then came NCAA tournament victories over Davidson (85-72) and North Carolina State (80-68) that vaulted them into the East Regional final against their lone conqueror, those pesky Wildcats of Villanova, at Carolina Coliseum in Columbia, S.C.

The day began so well. St. Bona, eager for revenge, pounced on the Wildcats early and led 46-30 at halftime. The rout continued into the second half and with 10 minutes left, the score had ballooned to 71-51. And then disaster struck.

Ford missed a shot from the lane, and when he went to follow it he tripped over someone's ankle and bowled into the side of Lanier's right knee, sending him sprawling to the floor in pain and St. Bona's championship hopes circling down the drain.

After a couple minutes Lanier rose, hobbled around a bit, and he looked as if he might be OK. In fact he convinced Weise to put him back into the game after a brief rest. But 34 seconds into that shift Lanier could play no longer, the pain too great, and he knew it was over.

"It sure doesn't feel like a win," Kull was heard to say amidst the silence in the St. Bona locker room. Another player murmured "We paid an awful price."

The next day, Lanier had his knee surgically repaired at Buffalo General Hospital. The good news was that the prog-

(St. Bonaventure University)

Billy Kalbaugh ran the offense for St. Bonaventure's great Final Four team in 1970, and he later returned to the school and served as an assistant coach under his old teammate, Jim Satalin.

nosis for a full recovery, and a future in the NBA, was a near certainty. The bad news: The Bonnies would have to go it alone against Jacksonville and it's twin seven-foot towers, Artis Gilmore and Pembrook Burrows.

"We're all going to have to do it," Kalbaugh said, speaking of filling the gaping void Lanier's absence was going to create. "We'll all have to hit the boards and score more. That's the way it has to be."

Said Weise: "This is a tough break for Bob and the team. But we're going to Maryland with a positive attitude. We've just got to work harder, everyone, including myself. We can't get down. We won't."

And they didn't. The Bonnies came out firing against Jacksonville. They raced to a 13-3 lead and a crowd of 14,380, clearly rooting for them, was electric. But then the officials started blowing a symphony with their whistles, and the Dolphins began a relentless parade to the foul line while Bona starters Gary and Gantt went to the bench. For the final nine minutes of the first half the Bonnies had a lineup on the floor that averaged barely six feet in height, while Jacksonville's front line averaged seven feet. Not surprisingly the Dolphins took a 42-34 lead into the break, and when they stretched it to 47-35 early in the second half, things looked bleak for the Bonnies.

Gantt fouled out with 10:45 to go, yet the Bonnies kept fighting and with 2:06 to go they were within 79-75 when Hoffman stole the ball and converted a layup. However, on the same play Hoffman was called for charging and while his basket counted, the Dolphins were awarded two free throws, and they made both. That was as close as it would get, and Jacksonville pulled away at the end for a 91-83 victory.

The Bonnies actually made seven more field goals, but in committing 32 personal fouls – which also cost them the services of Gary, Baldwin and Kull – they were outscored 37-15 at the line, and Weise was irate.

"I think (the officiating) was terrible for a tournament like this," he said. "There was a lot of terrible calls. There's no excuse for it. Our kids played their hearts out, I'm very proud of them."

Gilmore, a future ABA and NBA star, led the Dolphins with 29 points and 21 rebounds, but Burrows scored only five points. When Jacksonville coach Joe Williams said "We still would have beaten them with Lanier in the lineup" the reporters he was talking to had to bite their lips to keep from laughing.

So, what if?

"There's no doubt in my mind we would have won if we had Bob in the lineup," Weise said. "We would have won if Matt Gantt and Bubba Gary hadn't gotten into foul trouble. How can you foul out four men playing a zone?"

"The officiating stunk," added Kalbaugh. "The refs read that we weren't supposed to win and the refs made sure we didn't. We wanted to win so much for Bob. We knew missing this was hurting him so much. I know he feels as badly as we do. But we can walk with our heads up."

Thirty-three years later the pain lingers, the hearts have not mended, the tears have not dried. Time has not healed this wound.

"What we had was unique," Lanier said. "We shared so much together. We had no

---

BILLY KALBAUGH

Bob Lanier was the star, there was no denying that, and Kalbaugh understood what that meant for the 1969-70 St. Bonaventure team. "Hey, if you have a player like Bob Lanier on your team, you get him the ball," Kalbaugh said. "It doesn't take a genius to figure that out."

Nor does it take a genius to figure out how important Kalbaugh was to the success of the Bonnies that year. Kalbaugh almost always found a way to get Lanier the ball, but when he couldn't, Kalbaugh knew what to do with it.

Case in point was the Jacksonville game when Lanier wasn't there to take the ball. Kalbaugh scored 12 points against the Dolphins and he assisted on numerous baskets by Matt Gantt, Paul Hoffman and Vic Thomas, but it wasn't enough as the Bonnies fell, 91-83.

"Billy had complete command of our offense and he was as vital to our success as I was," Lanier once said.

A scorer in high school in Troy, N.Y., Kalbaugh was recruited by coach Larry Weise after he pumped in 56 points during a two-day tournament in Allentown, Pa. He made the all-tournament team along with a few guys named Calvin Murphy, Geoff Petrie and Jim McMillian, all of whom went on to star in the NBA. But when Kalbaugh came to Olean, Jim Satalin was the shooting guard, so Kalbaugh easily slipped into the point guard role.

"He had excellent court sense," Weise said. "As a player, all you had to do was tell him once and he'd have the whole situation in hand."

When Satalin became head coach at St. Bonaventure in 1973, he called Kalbaugh to serve as his top assistant coach, and it was Kalbaugh who recruited the likes of Earl Belcher and Glenn Hagan, two of the best players in school history.

"He's an excellent judge of talent," Satalin said. "Anyone can tell the great players. The key is picking the ones who in two years will be good players and fit into the system. Billy can pick those out."

In other words, players just like Kalbaugh.

---

egos. A little clip on the side (of his knee) ruined a beautiful dream."

Two days later a dejected St. Bona squad lost the meaningless consolation game to New Mexico State, 79-73, and UCLA went on to beat Jacksonville, 80-69, for the national championship. The Bonnies have played in the NCAA tournament just twice since, in 1978 and 2000, losing in the first round each time. Lanier recovered completely from his knee surgery and was taken No. 1 overall in the NBA draft by the Detroit Pistons. He went on to play 14 professional seasons, nine with Detroit, five with Milwaukee, and earned eight invitations to the NBA All-Star Game, winning MVP honors in the 1974 game. He finished his career with a 20.1 scoring

February 15, 1971 – Buffalo, N.Y.
Memorial Auditorium

Better Late Than Never

Randy Smith was arguably the greatest college athlete to ever compete for a Buffalo-area school as he earned All-American honors in three sports at Buffalo State College. There was one varsity basketball game that Smith did not start, though. After experiencing car trouble and arriving at the Aud just minutes before tip-off for the Bengals' game against arch-rival UB, Smith sat out the first seven minutes as punishment. However, he was on the floor at the end of the game, and his short jumper at the buzzer gave Buffalo State a narrow victory.

Randy Smith can't recall exactly why he and one of his Buffalo State teammates arrived at Memorial Auditorium just minutes before the start of the Bengals' annual alley fight against cross-town rival University of Buffalo in the winter of 1971.

And Smith, who would later play seven years at the Aud as a member of the NBA's Buffalo Braves, can't remember swishing an eight-foot put-back as the buzzer sounded to win the game for the Bengals that night, 87-85.

"But I do remember that I didn't start that game, and that was probably the only time I didn't start in my career, so I do remember that," Smith said.

No surprise there. Smith was then, and still is today, the greatest athlete to have ever worn the orange and black of Buffalo State. He was an All-American in basketball, soccer and track, and it was his standards by which all other athletes at the school were measured.

"During my time, there were two categories of athletes at Buffalo State," said Tony Sartori, who for more than 30 years was the school's primary athletic trainer. "There was Randy Smith and there were all the rest."

Smith always started, Smith always starred. He starred in this game against UB, scoring 24 points to help the Division II Bengals defeat their Division I counterparts for the sixth consecutive year. He did not, however, start.

Fifteen minutes before the tip-off the Bengals were going through warm-up drills and up in the stands where more than 3,200 had congregated, the murmuring began. Where's Randy? Buffalo State coach Don O'Brien was dying to know the answer to that question, too, but none was forthcoming so when it came time to hand in his starting lineup he was forced to do so without including Smith and fellow starter Glen Henley. Had O'Brien written their names down, and they didn't make it in time, the Bengals would have been assessed a technical foul.

"I guess we had car trouble and I forget how we got there," Smith said. "I knew that we were going to be late, but I thought we'd get there before tip-off, and we did. We got dressed quickly and we got out there just before the game started, but we didn't start, which I understood."

O'Brien not only didn't start the two players, he kept them glued to the bench for the first seven minutes of the game as a form of punishment, even though they had a perfectly good excuse for being tardy – car trouble on a snowy Buffalo night.

"He kept us out for seven minutes?" Smith asked rhetorically after being reminded of that fact. "Whoa, that's a long time, seven minutes. I guess he was making his point."

Point made, but O'Brien also realized the Bengals weren't going to beat the Bulls without Smith. O'Brien, in just his first year at the helm after taking over for longtime coach Howard MacAdam, had learned of Smith's value to the team very quickly.

Smith grew up on Long Island and at Bellport High he excelled in the three sports he would later play at Buffalo State. He had intrigued a handful of colleges, some were interested in him as a track athlete, others as a soccer player, and others as a basketball player. How he wound up on Elmwood Avenue was pure happenstance.

No one at Buffalo State knew who Smith was until he and the rest of New York state's finest high school track and field athletes convened at Buffalo State in the spring

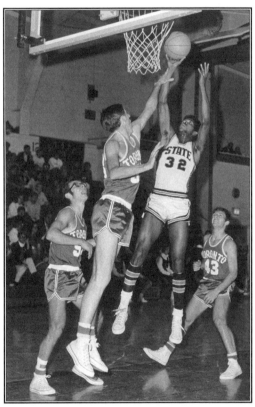

(Buffalo State College)

Randy Smith was a three-sport star at Buffalo State College who later went on to become one of the stalwarts of the Buffalo Braves, the city's NBA team that played at Memorial Auditorium from 1970-78. Smith remains Buffalo State's all-time leading scorer in basketball.

of 1967 for the state championships. Smith won the high-jump with a record leap, piquing the interest of Bengals' track coach Dick Marsh who was in attendance.

"I didn't know what Buffalo State was or where it was until I went there for that state track meet," Smith said. "Mr. Marsh and I talked and he sent the information back to me and we stayed in contact. He was responsible for me coming to school there, and he didn't even know about my soccer and basketball exploits."

Buffalo State and the rest of Western New York soon found out.

In addition to his track skills, Smith was also a dazzling soccer midfielder. He scored 40 career goals, a school record that was just broken in 1999, and in 1970 he led the Bengals into the NCAA tournament and a ranking of fifth in the nation. "I can't even tell you how many games we won 1-0 where he scored the only goal," Smith's soccer coach, Fred Hartrick said. "I think he could have been just as good a soccer player as he ended up being a basketball player at the pro level."

Perhaps, but it was hard to ignore his basketball achievements. By the time he graduated in 1971 Smith had scored a school-record 1,712 points without the benefit of four varsity seasons because freshmen were ineligible in those days. And with Smith leading the way, Buffalo State twice reached the NCAA small-college regionals, losing

---

CURTIS BLACKMORE

His is one of only three jerseys that hang from the rafters at UB's Alumni Hall, a number that will never again be worn by a Bulls' basketball player.

And to think, had it not been for coach Ed Muto, the civil unrest of the late 1960s likely would have prevented Blackmore from attending UB.

"There was a lot of turmoil on campus back in 1969 and '70," said Blackmore. "The atmosphere affected the whole athletic program. I was married and I didn't like what was happening around me. I thought about leaving. But coach talked not only with me but with my wife about the situation and was very reassuring. He showed us a lot of kindness. It meant a lot to me and we were friends throughout the rest of his life."

From 1970 to 1973 Blackmore was the dominant player for Muto's UB teams, a rebounding machine who still holds the school record for average rebounds per game in a season with 17.8 in 1972-73.

Blackmore, twice voted UB's most valuable player, ranks second on the school's all-time rebound list with 1,175 including a single-season standard of 427 set in 1972-73 when, in one game against Tennessee-Chattanooga, he pulled down 32, also still a record.

And he could score, too. The 1971-72 team which Blackmore anchored remains the highest-scoring UB club in history as it averaged 80.8 points per game. That year Blackmore averaged 18.7 points on his way to 1,287 career points which still puts him seventh on the Bulls' list. However, the six players ahead of him all had the benefit of four full varsity seasons. Blackmore played only three.

---

in the national semifinals in 1970, the year he averaged 25.6 points per game.

Smith was so good, the Buffalo Braves, in their second year as an NBA expansion team, drafted him in the seventh round. At first it was thought that the Braves were just trying to score some publicity points with the Buffalo fans. Soon, when Smith was outplaying the team's second-round draft choice, Grambling's Fred Hilton, in training camp, it was clear the Braves had unearthed a gem.

"We had talked to Howie MacAdam and we knew Randy was a super kid," said former St. Bonaventure coach and then-Braves general manager Eddie Donovan. "And he might be one of the best athletes who ever played the game. You have to take a chance with somebody like that. Did we know he was going to turn out like he did? If we did, we would have taken him a heckuva lot sooner than we did."

Joe Niland, who coached Canisius College in the early 1950s, didn't think Smith was ready for the NBA, and he shared his opinion with young Randy.

"He was trying to impress upon me that I should go over to Europe and play over there or play in the old Eastern League," Smith recalled. "He didn't think my skills were adequate enough to make the Braves in my first year. He wanted me to go get some more experience, but I proved them wrong. I told them 'No, I'm going to make the Braves.'"

He did, and he became one of the franchise's greatest players. The Braves have been gone for 25 years and are now the Los Angeles Clippers by way of San Diego, but Smith is still the franchise's all-time leader in games played, points, assists, steals, field goals attempted and made, and free throws attempted and made. He also played in 906 consecutive games which stood as the all-time NBA iron man record until A.C. Green broke the mark in 1997.

And to think, it all began at tiny Buffalo State. "I'm glad my coming to Buffalo worked out the way it did," he said. "Buffalo State gave me the opportunity and the people in Buffalo have always been great to me."

It was an affection borne out of respect for his talent, talent that was already in full bloom when he wore No. 32 for the Bengals.

Once Smith and Henley had paid their penance, O'Brien inserted both into the game which, at that juncture, had been a ragged and physical affair, each team scoring just seven points.

Immediately, Buffalo State's offense began to click and with Smith knocking down jumpers, the Bengals opened a six-point advantage. Behind the work of rugged center Curtis Blackmore, who would finish with 26 points and 20 rebounds, the Bulls forged ahead by four, and when the half ended, the score was tied for the ninth time at 37-37.

After intermission the Bengals took control and with Durie Burns (game-high 27 points plus 14 rebounds) outworking Blackmore at both ends, Smith and Henley chipping in with key baskets, and Ken Zak and George Holt creating havoc in Buffalo State's press, the Bengals opened a 74-61 lead with less than seven minutes remaining.

The issue appeared to be decided, but then UB coach Ed Muto sent Neil Langelier onto the floor, and the unheralded junior very nearly stole the game for the Bulls. He scored all 10 of his points during a 24-11 spurt, the last two coming on a 16-foot bank shot with 16 seconds remaining that produced an 85-85 tie.

"We were hoping for overtime," Muto said. "We had everything going our way in those late minutes."

What UB didn't have, though, was Smith.

After Buffalo State missed a game-winning shot, the ball went of bounds off a UB player with four seconds to go, so O'Brien called timeout to set up a play. Smith was the designated shooter, but the Bulls played strong defense and denied him the ball, so it wound up in Burns' hands. His shot clanged off the rim and Smith grabbed the rebound between two defenders, faked twice, then put up the follow shot that passed through the rim as the buzzer sounded.

"After battling Blackmore and having him on my back the whole night, I was too tired to have my shooting touch," Burns said. "We were lucky Randy was out far enough for that long rebound. A short one and it's overtime."

It's all a blur to Smith today, but outside of not starting, there was one other thing he remembered from that night.

"I always got full enjoyment out of beating UB," he said. "They were Division I and we were Division II, and they were our biggest rival."

Since retiring from the NBA in 1983, Smith has led an ever-changing life. He worked in real estate in Connecticut, and he came back to Buffalo to perform youth service and give birth to the Randy Smith League, a recreational summer basketball league that still thrives today. Later, he worked for the NBA helping counsel players, he coached in the CBA, and now, for the past seven years, he has worked as an executive for the Mohegan Sun Casino in Connecticut.

April 10, 1973 – Montreal, Quebec
The Forum

Thank You Sabres

He was often overshadowed by his French Connection linemates, Gilbert Perreault and Richard Martin, but Rene Robert was one of Buffalo's all-time clutch performers. He began to carve that reputation on an April night at the Montreal Forum in 1973 during the first NHL playoff series in Sabres history when he scored an overtime goal in Game 5 that briefly kept alive Buffalo's hopes for a stunning upset.

Y ou certainly couldn't blame Montreal Canadiens' center Peter Mahovolich for being a tad bit confident on the eve of the 1973 NHL playoffs.

The mighty Canadiens of Ken Dryden, Guy Lapointe, Guy Lafleur, Yvan Cournoyer, Jacques Lemaire and Henri Richard – losers of just 10 of 80 regular-season games – were matched up in the first round with the Buffalo Sabres, a franchise in its third year of existence playing in its first post-season series.

The Canadiens had practice pucks with more tradition than the Sabres, their stick boys had more experience than some of the Buffalo players. In fact, if you polled the Montreal roster it would not have been surprising if the majority of coach Scotty Bowman's boys thought Buffalo's team was still nicknamed the Bisons and playing in the American Hockey League.

"Really, I hope we don't win by big scores," Mahovolich said without a hint of arrogance in his voice the day before Game 1 at the Montreal Forum. "That hurts a team. I'd like to see 3-1 or 4-2 games where we're working all the time and not getting high on ourselves."

Oh, Mahovolich got his wish, and you can bet, upon reflection, he was none too happy about it.

After sweeping the first three games, the Canadiens were nearly pushed to the limit by the upstart Sabres, and by the time they had finally put away the series with a hard-fought 4-2 victory in Game 6 at Memorial Auditorium, they had seen more than enough of this young, energetic, soon-to-be Stanley Cup-contending Buffalo club.

"We played Buffalo in five good games during the season and I felt a lot of pressure in this series," Bowman admitted when it was over. ``I feel like somebody has just taken a piano off my back. No matter whom we face in the rest of the playoffs, they aren't going to be any tougher than the Sabres. This Buffalo team was badly underrated because it was only a third-year team."

The game that forever stamped the Sabres as a legitimate NHL franchise was Game 5 in Montreal, won by Buffalo 3-2 on Rene Robert's goal 9:18 into overtime. Thirty years have come and gone, but no Sabres' fan will ever forget Robert's slap shot skipping past Dryden, and the sight of the ghostly looks on the faces of the Canadiens as they watched the Sabres celebrate with unbridled glee on their hallowed ice.

It was Buffalo's first win in 11 tries at the Forum, and it came in the first overtime game in Sabres history. "All we wanted to do is prove to the world that we were a team on the upswing and we were there to stay, that we weren't a fluke," Robert recalled. "When we beat them in overtime, I think we opened a lot of eyes, especially because we beat them in Montreal."

Grinding left winger Craig Ramsay agreed.

"Game 5 was truly something special," Ramsay said. "When I saw Tim Horton

TIM HORTON

Thankfully, there was never a night quite like it in the history of the Buffalo Sabres. It was Feb. 21, 1974, and the Sabres were to play the Atlanta Flames at Memorial Auditorium just 15 hours after the death of their leader, their warrior, Horton.

The seemingly ageless 44-year-old defenseman had perished in a one-car accident in the pre-dawn hours while driving from Toronto to Buffalo on the Queen Elizabeth Way.

"I'll never forget the first game we played after he died," recalled Mike Robitaille, who like many in the usual sellout crowd stood there during the moment of silence with tears streaming down his face.

"It was an awful night to walk in and see his locker stall empty. You had a feeling like he was a safety net for all of us. When he walked in the dressing room everything was OK, Timmy's here. When he wasn't there, we were a little helter-skelter, you felt things could fall apart. He was the glue, just his presence, his past experience, and being the person that he was."

When police had arrived on the scene, they found coach Joe Crozier's phone number in Horton's wallet.

"When they called me to come down and identify the body, I couldn't believe that this could ever take place," Crozier said. "When I lost Tim Horton, damnit, I lost my heart."

Not to mention one of the greatest defenseman to ever play the game. During the 19 years he spent in Toronto the Leafs won four Stanley Cups – all teams coached by Punch Imlach – and Horton played in six All-Star games. After brief stints with the Rangers and the Penguins, Horton came to the Sabres before the 1972-73 season. Not surprisingly, that year Buffalo made it to the NHL playoffs for the first time, one year removed from having won just 16 games.

"He made the biggest impact in my life of anyone I've ever been involved with in hockey," said Robitaille. "I became an experienced player because of Tim, he was everything to me, my mentor, my hero. I idolized him. I used to stand at the blue line during warmups the way Tim did. He would stand there and take his one foot and bring the heel of his skate up, so I did the same thing just because Tim did."

His tenure in Buffalo was brief, but he was the player who taught the Sabres how to win.

and Roger Crozier, the way they played in that game, it was something that I'll never forget. I saw that night what veterans could do for a team and what it meant to have dedication and the willingness to go for it at all costs. Tim worked so hard and Roger was just unbeatable. I remember one shift late in the game, I was just exhausted, and I was out against the Cournoyer line and it was a shooting gallery in our end. I could barely put one foot in front of the other, and there's Timmy diving to block a shot, Roger knocking the puck away and making save after save. I'm thinking `If those guys can do it, I've got to find a way to do it, to play better. I've got to be better, I can't leave it all up to these guys.'"

Ramsay was not alone. That was the attitude of the entire team in the days leading up to the series opener. The Sabres had battled to the final night of the regular season to secure the last playoff berth in the Eastern Conference, and it took a 3-1 victory at the Aud over St. Louis to accomplish that goal. Coming off that high, the Sabres were caught up in a frenzy of foolhardiness, thinking they actually had a chance to beat Montreal.

"I'm not taking anything away from the Canadiens," coach Joe Crozier said. "They are without a doubt a super hockey club. But anything can happen in the playoffs. A team can get hot, a goaltender can get hot. I won't predict anything. The thing is, we're here because we deserve to be here. And we'd like to show everyone that."

Now, Robert smiles as he looks back on that pre-playoff exuberance. "When we played the Canadiens, let's be honest, we were hoping to play anyone but them that year," he said. "We were just hoping to do well. We knew our chances of beating them were very, very slim. They were so much more experienced and talented than we were all the way around."

Playing Montreal was tough enough, but to have to do it in the playoffs would be even more difficult, Ramsay recalled.

"I was a young guy, an intense guy, but I remember thinking 'We're in the playoffs against Montreal, how am I going to do this?'" Ramsay said. "`If this (the last game against St. Louis) was pressure, what's it going to be like in the playoffs?' Well, what happened is when we went in to play Montreal in that first game, I didn't feel pressure, I felt excitement. It was completely different, an incredible feeling and a

(Bill Wippert)

The most exciting sight at Memorial Auditorium on a nightly basis in the 1970s was Gilbert Perreault flying up and down the ice surface dazzling fans and opponents alike with his brilliance.

wonderful experience. That first game, we legitimately had a chance to win it."

In the opener, the Sabres outplayed Montreal only to lose 2-1 on Cournoyer's third-period power-play goal, and then in the next two games the Canadiens had done what everyone expected them to do – they dominated the Sabres in winning 7-3 and 5-2. However, the Sabres put together a strong Game 4 and coupled with a natural Montreal letdown, the result was Buffalo's inaugural playoff victory, 5-1.

"Give Buffalo credit, but this was a bad game for us, we got worse as we went along," Mahovolich said. "I don't think we'll repeat it."

They didn't. The Canadiens played like the Canadiens in Game 5. Only the Sabres played better.

In winning Game 4, Crozier had relied heavily on the French Connection line of Robert, Gilbert Perreault and Rick Martin. They produced 24 shots and combined to tally seven points with Perreault scoring twice and Robert once. So before the start of the fifth game, Crozier vowed to play the Connection all night if he had to.

"We'll win with Gil Perreault because that's the way we have to win," Crozier said. "He's the best player in the National Hockey League. We'll go with our best and I'll play the Perreault line as much as I can. We can play with the Montreal Canadiens, I believe it and my players believe it. And if the Perreault line is going, we'll beat them."

The Perreault line was going.

(Bill Wippert)

When Rene Robert (14) joined the Sabres late in the 1971-72 season, he proved right away that he would be a perfect fit on a line with Rick Martin and Gilbert Perreault. The following season, the French Connection was born.

And the Sabres beat them.

The Canadiens took a 1-0 lead at 16:22 of the first period when Frank Mahovolich beat Roger Crozier with a blast from just outside the blue line. The stout Montreal defense had contained The Connection throughout the opening period, and as a team, the Sabres had managed only six shots. However, Perreault was a whirling dervish in the middle period, and he set up a pair of goals that put Buffalo in front.

At 12:03 Robert stole a pass and sent Perreault and Martin in on a two-on-one break. Defenseman Serge Savard slid over to challenge Perreault, so Perreault slid a pass to Martin who fired a 15-foot wrist shot for the tying goal. Just 1:08 later, Perreault won a faceoff from Lemaire, the puck squirted to Robert in the slot, and he whipped a back-hander past Dryden from 20 feet and suddenly the Sabres were ahead, 2-1.

In the third the Canadiens began to feel a sense of urgency. They did not want to have to go back to Buffalo for a sixth game, and they came out determined to make sure that wasn't going to happen. One problem: Roger Crozier. He made 15 saves in the third period, and although he did allow the Canadiens to tie the game with 7:14 left when Richard set up Lapointe at the goal crease, he refused to let them win the game.

"It was a long night, even before we went into overtime," Roger said that night. "The Canadiens never let up, they just keep coming. But our team played well. When you consider the pressure on these guys we have who haven't been in the Stanley Cup playoffs before, you have to say they played exceptionally well. The type of club Montreal is, you have to be at the peak of your game to beat them. And in overtime, that's especially tough."

Just before regulation time ran out, Joe Crozier called referee Bruce Hood over to the Buffalo bench to make an unusual request. He wanted Hood to measure the width of Dryden's leg pads because he knew they were wider than the mandated 10 inches.

Buffalo's public relations director, Paul Wieland, had told Crozier almost a month earlier that he suspected the pads were illegal. Crozier and general manager Punch Imlach sat on the information, then had Wieland sneak into the Canadiens locker room at the Aud prior to the start of Game 3, and sure enough Wieland found them to be a shade wider than 10 inches.

The penalty for illegal goalie pads was a two-minute minor to be assessed at the start of the next period. Crozier and Imlach agreed to use the loophole to their advantage in a tie game near the end of regulation, so the Canadiens would have to start the over-time period shorthanded. That scenario did not present itself in Game 3, and the Sabres didn't need any help in Game 4. But with 29 seconds to go in Game 5, the time was right.

"When Joe called the pads on Dryden, that was great because I thought Bowman's head was going to explode," Martin recalled with a laugh. "Whatever hair he had on his head, he was pulling it out, and Joe just stood there smiling. That was just beautiful. We were laughing our asses off."

The Sabres' plan almost had a storybook conclusion when, on the ensuing power play to start the extra period, Jim Lorentz came within inches of ending the game.

However his shot clanged off the goal post, and Montreal was able to ward off any further threats and killed the penalty. In a way, it was probably appropriate that the Sabres didn't score on that power play because there is no question many people would have considered the victory tainted.

Although they didn't score, the Sabres were in control because The Connection was flying. Just before the start of the overtime Joe Crozier had pulled aside Perreault and said "You're better than anyone they've got on the ice, Gil. You can win this hockey game for me. Just take that puck and go through them all."

It didn't quite work out that way, but Perreault did make the pass that sent Robert in for the breakaway that resulted in the winning goal.

"The play developed in Rick's corner," Robert said recounting the momentous goal. "One of the defenseman (Jim Schoenfeld) pinched in, and Gilbert was able to get loose, and by the time he got loose, I had beaten Savard on the far side. When Gilbert saw me, he gave me a hard pass, and I knew once I got the puck nobody could catch me. I knew what I wanted to do, I was just hoping I could do it. I saw the opening, I had about a foot and a half to shoot at (on Dryden's stick side) and I knew from past experiences if you faked him high, he had a tendency of twitching and pulling up, so what I did was shoot the puck along the ice and he just had no chance. It was an absolutely perfect shot."

For the first time all season, the Canadiens had lost two games in a row, and as the Sabres packed their gear for the flight back to Buffalo – where they would be greeted in the early morning by about 500 delirious fans – people were daring to believe that maybe that youthful foolhardiness the players had exuded before the series began wasn't so foolhardy. Maybe the Sabres could win this series.

"Montreal was under pressure to take four straight from us and when they won the first three, the heat had to be off a little," captain Gerry Meehan said upon returning to Buffalo. "Now that we have won two in a row, the pressure has to be back on them to take the series. I think we'll be going back to Montreal (for Game 7)."

There was no return to Montreal as the Canadiens took care of business in Buffalo, scoring four first-period goals and then holding on for a 4-2 series-clinching victory. They ultimately defeated Chicago in six games to win the Stanley Cup. As the clock in the Aud ticked off the final minute of this glorious season, the fans in the sold-out arena chanted "Thank You Sabres, Thank You Sabres" providing a never-to-be-forgotten moment in Buffalo sports history. "We had tried so hard, it was such a great year, and when the fans chanted `Thank You Sabres' it was so incredibly moving," said Ramsay. "It was truly a very special experience to be in that building that night. We were on the bench saying `What is this? Can you believe this? Is this the greatest?' We came out of that game feeling awful that we had lost, but we also felt how great it was to be in Buffalo, how great it was to be in this city, playing for this team in this building."

December 16, 1973 – New York City
Shea Stadium

Two Grand

We no longer remember O.J. Simpson as the great football star that he was, and
you would be hard-pressed to find someone who has fallen farther from grace than
the Juice. But once upon a time Simpson was an icon, Buffalo's lightning rod to the
big time. He ran through defenses just as easily as he ran through airports in his
Hertz commercials, and in 1973, he entered uncharted NFL territory when he
became the first player to surpass 2,000 yards rushing in a single season.

On the morning of the Buffalo Bills' 1973 season finale, O.J. Simpson awoke from a
restless night of attempted sleep with a terrible thought on his mind.

Looking out of a New York City hotel room window and seeing snow falling on
Gotham, he turned to his roommate and best friend, offensive guard Reggie McKenzie,
and said "Reg, what if I only get 40 yards?"

McKenzie – a second-year pro who Simpson called "my main man" – looked at
the man he called "Juice," the man who was on the verge of football immortality, and
rolled his eyes and said "There's no way that's gonna happen. We're gonna win and
you're gonna get Brown's record. I can feel it in my bones."

It was as if the bombastic McKenzie had provided a security blanket. Simpson,
who later that day would attempt to break the great Jim Brown's single-season NFL
rushing record, instantly relaxed. Of course Reggie was right, Simpson thought to himself. He was just 60 yards shy of the mark, and he talked himself into believing he could
get that in one quarter under the right circumstances.

When Simpson arrived in the dingy visitors' locker room at Shea Stadium a few
hours later, he received further comfort from the members of the Bills' offensive line,
affectionately known as "The Electric Company" because they turned on the juice.

"When the ball is snapped," tackle Dave Foley said, clapping Simpson on the
back, "just follow us." Added McKenzie: "Climb right up my back if you have to."

Just two years previous, Simpson had completed his third consecutive unproduc-
tive season with the Bills and the No. 1 overall pick in the 1969 draft was beginning to
look like a colossal bust. During those three forgettable years Buffalo had won just 8 of
42 games and Simpson – plagued by injuries and a lack of talent around him – had
gained only 1,927 yards rushing and was privately questioning his football future.

And then, as if sent from the heavens above, came Lou Saban, the coach who had
led the Bills to back-to-back AFL championships in 1964 and '65, and was now being
re-hired by team owner Ralph Wilson and charged with restoring the laughable Bills to
their past glory.

"I believe in running the ball, basic, hard-nosed football," Saban said when he was re-introduced to the Buffalo media. "We have a great runner, a game-breaker who is a great athlete, and I intend to use him."

Simpson won the NFL's rushing title in 1972 with 1,251 yards, and now in 1973, his career in total resurrection, Simpson had already secured another rushing crown, having piled up 1,803 rushing yards in 13 games.

Exactly 11 years and one day earlier, when Simpson was a teenager growing up in San Francisco, he had sidled up to Brown in a soda shop near Kezar Stadium after Brown's Cleveland Browns had defeated the 49ers to close the 1962 NFL season. The brash kid said to the superstar "When I'm a pro I'm gonna break all your records."

Simpson didn't break all of Brown's records, but before the first quarter was through in what became a 34-14 Buffalo victory over the New York Jets, Simpson shattered Brown's most coveted record. He followed McKenzie and the Bills' other guard,

(Robert L. Smith)

O.J. Simpson's was starting to look like a first-round bust until Lou Saban returned to Buffalo in 1972 and resurrected his career. With Saban's run-oriented approach, Simpson became the first back in NFL history to surpass 2,000 yards rushing in a single season.

Joe DeLamielleure, through the left side of the line on a play called "27" for a six-yard gain, and that run vaulted Simpson past the man he would later join in the Pro Football Hall of Fame.

The appreciative New York crowd gave Simpson a standing ovation. Referee Bob Frederic presented him with the ball he had carried on the record-breaking play. And his teammates hugged him and congratulated him. One particular teammate, though, wasn't satisfied. "Juice, job's not done, got lots of work to do," McKenzie said. McKenzie wanted 2,000 yards, perhaps even more than Simpson.

JOE DELAMIELLEURE

It shouldn't have come down to a full-court press applied by the Bills' public relations department to get Joe D. elected to the Pro Football Hall of Fame.

During his 13-year NFL career, the first seven of which were spent in Buffalo, DeLamielleure established himself as one of the finest offensive guards to ever play the game. Too bad the voters for the Hall of Fame didn't readily recognize what DeLamielleure's peers always knew.

But in an effort to right this wrong, the Bills put together a packet of information to help educate the voters, and they finally saw the light. Once they realized that Joe D. started 64 more NFL games than fellow guard and 1987 inductee Jim Langer, and that no less than Mean Joe Greene once said that

"No one blocked me better than Joe DeLamielleure" the voters came to their senses and made him part of the 2003 class.

Reggie McKenzie may have been O.J. Simpson's "main man" during the Juice's glory days in Buffalo, but DeLamielleure was O.J.'s best blocker. He had the speed to pull out on sweeps and the strength to stand toe-to-toe in pass blocking situations against any defensive player.

"He was the best offensive guard I ever coached," said Jim Ringo, the former Green Bay great and ex-Bills head coach and offensive line coach who himself is a Hall of Famer. "He did it the way it was supposed to be done, without mistakes."

Deacon Jones, the Hall of Fame defensive end of the Los Angeles Rams, had never bought into the theory that Simpson had lost the greatness he had displayed collegiately at USC when he won the Heisman Trophy in 1968. After Simpson's third year with the Bills, Jones said "He's a great runner, but by the time Buffalo gets enough good players around him, he might be punch-drunk. If he were with us, he'd gain 2,000 yards."

Forget Los Angeles. As far as McKenzie was concerned, the 2,000-yard threshold was reachable right here in Buffalo, and he'd said so long before Simpson had begun his quest. "I told O.J. during the summer 'Let's shoot for two grand and really set the world on fire'" McKenzie recalled.

Simpson laughed it off at the time during training camp at Niagara University. McKenzie wasn't laughing on the practice field then, and he wasn't laughing now amidst the swirling snow and cold mud of Shea Stadium, at least not until 5:56 remained in the game when McKenzie led Simpson around left tackle for a seven-yard gain that pushed the "Juice" past the never-before-broken barrier.

In an interview that was conducted in 1994 – just nine days before his ex-wife, Nicole, and her friend, Ron Goodman, were murdered in Los Angeles, a double-homicide for which Simpson was tried for and ultimately acquitted of – Simpson remembered the excitement he had felt heading into the 1973 season. "If I could lead the league in rushing with the team we had in 1972, I knew that if we improved the talent, I could do a lot better," Simpson said. "By the time we got to training camp in 1973, I saw an offense that I knew could be formidable."

But no one could have foreseen that the Bills would be as formidable as they were. Simpson exploded for an NFL-record 250 yards against New England on opening day, and so began a 14-week odyssey that even now, 30 years later, seems almost mythical.

Simpson was on pace for the previously unimagined 2,000 as he topped 1,000 yards in the seventh game against Kansas City, which happened to be Buffalo's first appearance on *Monday Night Football*. The charge was slowed in the next two weeks as New Orleans (79) and Cincinnati (99) held him under 100 yards. He got back on track with 124 yards against the Colts and 137 against Atlanta, but with 1,584 yards through 12 games, it was now going to take a huge effort just to catch Brown in the last two games because he was 279 yards shy of the former Cleveland star's mark.

However, on a snow-covered Rich Stadium field in Week 13, Simpson skated through the Patriots for 219 yards, giving him a league-record 10 100-yard games in one season, and leaving him just 60 yards away from Brown, 197 from 2,000.

Simpson carried on seven of eight plays on Buffalo's opening possession against the Jets, gaining 57 yards to set up Jim Braxton's one-yard TD plunge for a 7-0 lead.

On the play after he broke Brown's record, Simpson lost a fumble, and the Jets turned that into the tying score as Joe Namath fired a 48-yard TD pass to Jerome Barkum.

But this was Simpson's day, Buffalo's day. He broke a 13-yard touchdown run with 1:12 left in the first half, and after the Jets went three-and-out on their ensuing series, Buffalo's Bill Cahill fielded Julian Fagin's low punt and roared right up the middle for a 51-yard touchdown return to give the Bills a 21-7 halftime lead.

With Simpson needing 90 yards to reach 2,000, the Bills continued to feed him the ball in the second half, but during the third quarter, the Jets defense suddenly stiffened. They had allowed Simpson to break Brown's record, but they didn't want insult added to injury by letting him reach 2,000.

The Bills tacked on another touchdown plunge by Braxton and a field goal by John Leypoldt to increase their lead to 31-7, and while Simpson was inching closer to

2,000, it was beginning to look like he wasn't going to make it.

So Ferguson entered the huddle and delivered a progress report on just exactly how close Simpson was to 2,000. Dutifully fired up, The Electric Company turned it up a notch and blew the Jets out of the way. After a five-yard gain by Simpson, Ferguson knew the record was near, and when he looked to the sideline, he found out how near. Someone was holding up four fingers, so he called Simpson's number one last time, and when New York safety Phil Wise tackled him seven yards downfield, history had been made.

Afterward a special interview room was set up to deal with the overflow media, and rather than meet the press alone, Simpson brought in the entire offensive unit and introduced them one-by-one. "These are the cats who did it," he said. "They worked for it all year. Getting the record meant a lot to me, personally. Just two years ago I was as low as I could be, so you will never realize just how much this means to me."

Simpson's record stood for 11 years until Eric Dickerson of the Los Angeles Rams broke it, and since then, Denver's Terrell Davis and Detroit's Barry Sanders have joined the 2,000-yard club. However, Simpson is the only member to have done it in a 14-game season. And it turned out that Simpson wasn't anywhere close to being as low as he could be. Simpson was charged with the double murder in June 1994 in Los Angeles, and despite seemingly overwhelming evidence against him, he was found innocent by a jury in October 1995 in one of the most celebrated trials in United States history. "You'll never be able to hear O.J. Simpson's name or even watch the great vintage footage of O.J. Simpson as one of the very greatest players who ever lived without thinking of this tragedy," said broadcaster Bob Costas, who worked on NBC's NFL studio show with Simpson. "But that's the consequence of what happened."

April 12, 1974 – Buffalo, N.Y.
Memorial Auditorium

The Foul

Playoff heartbreak has become a staple of life for the Buffalo sports fan. Lost among the various postseason misdeeds of the Bills and Sabres – four straight Super Bowl losses and two Stanley Cup Finals defeats just to scratch the surface – are the now defunct Buffalo Braves who endured a crushing six-game series loss to the Boston Celtics in the 1974 NBA playoffs.

All they could do was stand there and watch, and that's what made it so painful for the Buffalo Braves.

Brilliant Bob McAdoo couldn't rise up and block a shot, Gar Heard or Jim McMillian couldn't play suffocating defense, and Ernie DiGregorio or Randy Smith couldn't make a steal and start a fastbreak the other way.

All they could do was stand there and watch, hands on hips, helpless, hopeless, as Boston's Jo Jo White toed the free-throw line at Memorial Auditorium poised to bring to an end not only Game 6 of this NBA Eastern Conference semifinal playoff series, but the Braves' season. "It's one thing to lose," Buffalo reserve guard Kenny Charles said afterward. "It's another thing to lose like that."

Long before "Wide Right" and "No Goal" and "Music City Miracle" there was "The Foul." It is largely forgotten today because the Braves left town in 1978 and over the past quarter of a century their once-vibrant existence has faded into the deepest recesses of the Buffalo sports fans' mind.

But at the time, the Braves' 106-104 loss to the Celtics – when White sank two controversial free throws with no time remaining on the clock to end the game and the series – enraged Buffalonians, turned coach Jack Ramsay's face fire engine red, and prompted team owner Paul Snyder and general manager Eddie Donovan to send a telegram to the NBA office in New York City announcing their intention to formally protest the grim result.

"I can't believe it's over," Buffalo's Jack Marin said that night. To this day, if you polled every Brave who was in uniform, they'd say it never was over, it still isn't over. The Braves, who were trailing three games to two in the first postseason series in the team's four-year history, had battled back from a 97-88 deficit with 5:45 left in the fourth quarter, and thanks to McAdoo's slam dunk off a steal, were tied with the mighty Celtics at 104 with seven seconds left in regulation.

The Aud – filled to the rafters with 18,237 rabid partisans, the largest basketball gathering ever assembled in the building – trembled with excitement as the Celtics prepared to take the ball out at mid-court following a timeout.

Not a seat was occupied, and the din emanating from the arena probably caused ripples out on bordering Lake Erie as super Celtic John Havlicek took Don Nelson's inbounds pass and worked his way into position near the top of the key for a shot. Just as he let it go McAdoo rose up and deflected it, but the ball caromed directly to White 20 feet from the basket. The Boston guard, knowing the clock was speeding toward zero, quickly fired up a jumper of his own. McAdoo, who seemed to be everywhere in the final minutes, somehow got back into the play, but in his attempt to block White's heave, he fouled him.

On this there was no debate, save for McAdoo who said "Hell no" when asked whether he clipped White. But there was a foul. The Celtics knew it, the officials knew it, and the Braves admitted it.

However, as White's shot bounced off the left side of the rim, and referee Darrel Garretson raised his right arm to signal the foul, the clock inexplicably ran out and the horn sounded. At that moment, chaos reigned as the Braves vehemently argued that there was at least one second – perhaps two – on the clock when Garretson called the foul.

After a lengthy discussion, Garretson, his referee partner Mendy Rudolph, and reserve official Manny Sokol who was sitting at the scorers' table, determined that the clock had indeed expired and there would be no further play after White's free throws, unless he some-how managed to miss all three he had been awarded under the old three shots to make two rule.

Ramsay went ballistic, repeat-edly thrusting his arm skyward and pointing to the clock on the big blue scoreboard that hung above the floor. The Braves threw their arms up in dis-gust. The fans rained everything from beer cups – some empty, some full – to rolled up programs onto the shiny hardwood. And Boston coach Tommy Heinsohn wore the look of the cat who'd just eaten the canary.

"It was a hell of a gutsy call by the official, but it was the right call," Heinsohn said. "The ball hit the rim, came off it, and it was at zero."

That wasn't Ramsay's take. "It's ridiculous to end a game and a series on a call like that, a borderline call,"

(Courier-Express)

Despite the heroics of Bob McAdoo, the Braves simply weren't good enough to get past Boston in the first round of the 1974 playoffs and lost a hard-fought six-game series.

Dr. Jack said. "If the foul occurred before time ran out, then we had whatever time was left after he blew the whistle. And if Mac hit Jo Jo after time ran out, it shouldn't have counted."

Even White conceded that the Braves probably deserved at least a second.

"McAdoo definitely fouled me, and when I hit the floor I saw one second on the clock and then I heard the whistle," said the classy White. "I expected the foul to be called, but I don't think the timekeeper did. That's why he let the second go and the game ended."

(Courier-Express)

After losing at least 60 games in their first three NBA seasons, the Braves were revitalized in 1973 with the arrival of first-round draft choice Ernie DiGregorio. In his first year Ernie D. led the Braves to a 42-40 record and a playoff berth, along the way winning the NBA Rookie of the Year award.

With the fans erupting all around him, White missed the first free throw, bringing a huge roar. But he calmly hit the second to secure the victory, and then made the third for good measure. "I wasn't worried after I missed the first shot," said White, who finished with 18 points. "I had two left and if I ever miss three foul shots in a situation like that, I'll have to hang 'em up."

In those days when teams that were in relative close proximity met in the playoffs, home games were rotated, so the 56-26 Celtics enjoyed the home-court advantage over the 42-40 Braves in the odd-numbered games. Predictably, Boston won all three games at Boston Garden by scores of 107-97, 120-107 and 100-97, but Buffalo had taken Games 2 and 4 at the Aud, 115-105 and 104-102.

Early on in Game 6 it looked as if the home-court pattern would continue as Buffalo raced to a 16-6 lead and only the outside shooting of Havlicek (30 points), who drained four long bombs, prevented a quick blowout. Boston had the better of play in the second period as reserve guard Paul Westphal poured in 12 points, but Smith's steal and dunk just before the buzzer gave the Braves a 54-53 halftime lead. In the third quarter, McAdoo and DiGregorio combined for 22 points, but Havlicek and White matched them, and with the rest of the Celtics owning a 12-6 edge, Boston took an 87-82 lead into the final 12 minutes.

Midway through the third period Heinsohn took Don Chaney out of the game and moved Havlicek into the backcourt to play alongside White and that's when the Celtics began taking control. "Things began to happen," McMillian said. "The ball was moving better, the ball was getting up court quicker and the guards were getting good shots. When you have a backcourt of Havlicek and White, that's tough."

With 5:45 left and the Braves down 97-88, McAdoo took the game over. His 10 points keyed a 16-7 run that evened the count, the last four coming off Boston turnovers. With 17 seconds left and the Celtics leading 104-100, McMillian missed a short jumper and Boston rebounded, but Marin picked off a pass near midcourt and he fed McAdoo for a layup with 10 seconds to go. On the ensuing inbounds play, Dave Cowens fumbled Nelson's pass, McAdoo grabbed the ball and steamed in for the tying dunk.

"The pass was too hard and it went right through Cowens' hands and I was right there," McAdoo said. The basket gave McAdoo 40 points and the Braves new life, short-lived as it was.

ERNIE DIGREGORIO

He made the game look so easy with his effortless dribbling, his artistic passing and his silky-smooth shooting touch, but it was never easy for Ernie D.

Even as an All-American point guard at Providence, being 5-foot-11 and slow was a hindrance and those gym-rat hours he used to keep were out of necessity more than anything else.

It worked for a little while. DiGregorio was selected No. 3 overall by the Braves in the 1973 draft and went on to win NBA rookie of the year honors as he averaged 15 points and 8.2 assists per game and made 90.2 percent of his free throws to lead the league in helping the Braves reach the playoffs for the first time.

"Ernie was terrific his rookie year," said Braves coach Jack Ramsay.

However, a knee injury early in his second year pretty much scuttled DiGregorio's career. He was never the same. He played just 31 games in 1974-75 and missed the entire postseason, and he shared time with Kenny Charles the next year. In 1976-77 he regained his starting job and he won another free-throw shooting crown, but the Braves won only 30 games, missed the playoffs, and in the off-season, they gave up on Ernie D.

He played for the Lakers and eventually, he ended his NBA career with the Celtics in 1978, retiring at the age of 27.

"It was hard for me to accept the fact that I couldn't play in the NBA anymore," DiGregorio said. "I had put a lot of time and heart into the game. And I got a lot out of it."

Just not nearly as much as he – or anyone in Buffalo who saw him play in that magical rookie season – expected.

The next day the Braves were informed that their formal protest was being denied by the NBA, even though Donovan produced video showing one second remaining on the clock when White hit the deck. "The pictures are fact, not interpretation," Donovan said. "There was at least one second left, possibly two. It definitely should have been played." The Celtics came away from the series duly impressed by the young Braves. "I know they're disappointed, but they should be congratulated," said Havlicek. "They have a great future and should have lots of confidence for the upcoming years." McAdoo, who won the first of his three consecutive regular-season scoring titles with a 30.6 average in 1973-74, surpassed that mark in the six-game series, averaging 33.3, prompting Boston's Paul Silas to say "McAdoo's a heck of a player." The Celtics went on to defeat the New York Knicks in five games to win the East, and then beat the Milwaukee Bucks of Kareem Abdul-Jabbar and Oscar Robertson in a thrilling seven-game NBA championship series, their first title since 1968-69.

April 18, 1975 – Buffalo, N.Y.
Memorial Auditorium

108-102,Fifty Points for McAdoo

*In the mid-1970s, there were very few cities who could boast of the superstar
athletic talent of Buffalo. There was O.J. Simpson of the Bills, Gilbert Perreault
of the Sabres, and Bob McAdoo of the Braves, and all three ended up in their
respective sports' halls of fame. Because basketball wasn't as popular among the
fans as football and hockey, and because McAdoo's stay in Buffalo was compara-
tively short, he sometimes does not get his just due. But he was the talk of the town
the night he scored 50 points to lead the Braves to a thrilling playoff victory over
the Washington Bullets.*

All the Buffalo Braves and the National Basketball Association wanted to do was give
Bob McAdoo – to borrow a term from today's vernacular – his props.

All the superstar center wanted to do was go to the center circle, win the opening
jump ball, and get the Braves' playoff game against the Washington Bullets underway.

"I appreciated it," McAdoo said of the short ceremony that was held before the
teams took the Memorial Auditorium court in Game 4 of their 1975 Eastern Conference
semifinal so that NBA deputy commissioner Simon Gourdine could present McAdoo
with the league's MVP trophy which he so richly deserved.

"But I wanted to get the game started and over with. I usually can't wait for the
national anthem and the introductions to get over so we can start, especially in the playoffs. They're tough for me, I don't sleep and eat right because I'm always thinking about
the games."

McAdoo did most of his game-related pondering pre-tip as he would pore over
scouting reports and think about how he was going to attack that night's opponent. But
it's a safe bet to assume that he did plenty of thinking about this particular game long
after the final horn sounded and Buffalo had rung up a 108-102 victory before 15,307
exhilarated patrons.

McAdoo, who led the league in scoring during the regular season with a 34.5
average, exploded for 50 points and pulled down 21 rebounds, the greatest single-game
performance in the Braves' much-too-short eight-year tenure in Buffalo.

"It just happened," McAdoo said with a shrug of his shoulders. "I had an advantage in size over (Mike) Riordan when he was guarding me."

McAdoo had an advantage over everyone who was guarding him. Bullets coach
K.C. Jones had said earlier in the series that one of the keys to containing McAdoo was
to run a "fresh face" at him all night.

But no matter who was assigned to check him, all McAdoo was saying was "In
your face." Jones' defensive rotation included Riordan, Wes Unseld, Elvin Hayes, Nick

Weatherspoon and Tom Kozelko, and McAdoo schooled every one of them in turning in one of the finest playoff efforts in NBA history.

"Put that camera on Mac and he goes," Braves' reserve forward Paul Ruffner said, referring to the game being televised nationally by CBS.

The Braves on national television? It didn't seem possible during the first three years of the team's existence. Buffalo was awarded an NBA franchise in time for the 1970-71 season, but the team was anything but NBA caliber in posting records of 22-60, 22-60 and 21-61 its first three years. The only thing preventing three straight last-place finishes in the Atlantic Division was the historic 9-73 calamity that was the Philadelphia 76ers in 1972-73, still the worst record in NBA history.

Things had begun to turn for the Braves that year when Dr. Jack Ramsay was hired as coach and they selected McAdoo in the first round of the NBA draft and watched him earn the league's rookie of the year award. Then in 1973 they added to the largess by choosing play-making guard Ernie DiGregorio in the first round of the draft to pair with up-and-coming shooting guard Randy Smith, and forwards Jim McMillian and Gar Heard were acquired in trades about a month before the start of the regular season.

With DiGregorio following in McAdoo's footsteps by winning the rookie of the year award (he led the league in assists and free throw shooting percentage), and McAdoo capturing the first of his three straight scoring titles (30.6), the Braves doubled their win total to 42 and made their first playoff appearance. Though Boston knocked the Braves out, the series was a surprisingly hard-

(Courier-Express)

Bob McAdoo led the NBA in scoring three straight years while playing for the Braves, including a 34.5 average during the 1974-75 season. His 50-point effort against the Washington Bullets in Game Four was the all-time Braves record, but Buffalo still lost the series in seven games.

fought six-game battle.

Buffalo had high hopes for 1974-75, especially when it ran off a team-record 11-game winning streak in November to zoom to the top of the division standings. The good fortune did not last as Boston, after a middling 11-10 start, won 49 and lost only 12 the rest of the way, winning 18 of 19 games in one stretch. Meanwhile, the Braves managed 49 wins, a team record, and quite an accomplishment given that Ernie D missed most of the season with a knee injury, McMillian sat out 20 games with an illness, and Heard missed 15 with an ankle injury. McAdoo was the rock. Every night, even though opponents knew he was the primary offensive weapon and did everything they could to stop him, no one could.

And he saved his best for what to this point was Buffalo's biggest game of the season. The Braves won the opener at the Capital Centre, 113-102, then lost at the Aud, 120-106, and again back in Washington, 111-96. As Heard said of Game 4, "This was a game that we had to have. If we lost, the series would have been just about over."

Buffalo sputtered early and Washington had the better of play in taking a 25-23

(Courier-Express)

Jack Ramsay turned the Braves' fortunes around and guided the team in the playoffs three years in a row, then left following the 1976 season and the next year, coached the Portland Trail Blazers to the NBA championship.

lead through one quarter. McAdoo opened his scoring barrage with 10 points, then had another 10 in the second quarter, but it mattered little as the Bullets stretched their advantage to 56-47 at the break. It was an ominous position for the Braves because in their two losses, the games had been decided by Buffalo's inadequate third-quarter play. "We lost the last two games in the third quarter, so we were determined to go out and catch up in the third quarter," McAdoo said. "Once we caught 'em, we weren't going to let them pass us."

The Braves outscored Washington 31-19 in the third as McAdoo took over the game scoring 15 points and hauling in 10 rebounds. It was McAdoo's jumper from the left corner with 3:05 left in the period that put the Braves ahead for good at 70-68, and they entered the final 12 minutes clinging to a 78-75 lead.

The Bullets, who had tied Boston for the best regular-season record at 60-22, were within 82-81 early in the fourth, but a 14-5 Buffalo run over the next five minutes made it 96-86. A key moment in that spurt came with 6:22 remaining and Buffalo lead-

JACK RAMSAY

Ramsay obviously has fond recollections of his days as head coach in Portland because, after all, he led the Blazers to an NBA championship in 1977. However, Dr. Jack has never forgotten the four years he spent coaching the Buffalo Braves.

Ramsay took a young franchise that had won just 26 percent of its games during its first three years of existence – including a 21-61 mark his first year in 1972-73 – and led it to three consecutive playoff appearances between 1974 and '76.

"I enjoyed my time in Buffalo," said Ramsay, now an analyst for ESPN. "I liked the team except for the first year. The first year was painful. There just wasn't the personnel you needed to compete in the NBA. The second year we changed nine players and doubled our win production. That was the team that I liked. The next three years were fun years. But it was not a team that could win the championship.

"We really didn't have any veteran players. We ran the ball. We really pushed it. We basically tried to outscore the other guys. That's not a good premise. You're not going to win a championship with that. But it was a fun team. We scored a lot of points and won a lot of games."

Though Ramsay left for Portland following the 1976 playoff loss to Boston and struck gold in Oregon, he was disappointed by the implosion of the Braves.

"When I left the team, it was pretty good," Ramsay said of the '76 Braves. "But when I left, the owner (Paul Snyder) sold players. He got rid of McMillian, McAdoo and other reserves. The team took a nose dive. He tore the team up. Then after selling the players, he sold the team to John Y. Brown. From that day until the present, they've been scrambling to get a team together."

ing by just six. Hayes, the Bullets' leading scorer who had been held to one basket in the second half by Heard, fouled out.

"I got a lot of help from our guards," said Heard of his stifling defense on the Big E. "I played him in front. They had to get the ball high to get it over me. Usually by the time Hayes got it there was someone else there to help me out."

McAdoo was more impressed by Heard's work than he was his own. "We wouldn't have won without Gar's great defensive job on Hayes," he said. "Hayes' foul trouble was a big factor."

Frustrated by referee Richie Powers, Bullets assistant coach Bernie Bickerstaff drew a double technical and an ejection with a minute left, and by sinking one of the free throws, McAdoo reached the 50-point plateau. He then left the game to a standing ovation, and when the final horn sounded, some fans were heard to be chanting "108-102, 50 points for McAdoo."

Nearly an hour later, after a shower and a session with the media, McAdoo took hold of his MVP trophy and walked out of the building. But on this night, it was McAdoo who should have been carried out – on the shoulders of the celebrating fans.

Washington ultimately won the series, but it needed all seven games. The Bullets won Game 5 by 97-93, lost Game 6 at the Aud, 102-96, then ran away in Game 7 by 115-96. The Bullets wound up reaching the NBA Finals where they lost to Rick Barry and Golden State. The Braves made it to the playoffs for the third straight year in 1975-76 and finally won their first series, eliminating Philadelphia in a three-game first-round test. However, the rival Celtics were waiting in the Eastern Conference semifinals, and Boston survived another bitter battle with Buffalo to win four games to two. Then it all fell apart for the Braves. Ramsay bolted town to become head coach in Portland, and while he was leading the Trail Blazers to the NBA championship in his first year, the Braves slumped to 30-52 under Tates Locke, Bob MacKinnon and Joe Mullaney. Cotton Fitzsimmons took over in 1977-78, but he managed just a 27-55 record in front of dwindling Aud crowds. That led to one of the strangest transactions in pro sports history. Impatient new Braves owner John Y. Brown – who had purchased the team from Paul Snyder – and Celtics owner Irv Levin bought each other's teams, and Levin promptly moved the Braves to San Diego where they became the Clippers. Pro basketball has never returned to Western New York.

May 20, 1975 – Buffalo, N.Y.
Memorial Auditorium

Whistling Through the Graveyard

First a bat found its way into the Aud and pestered fans and players alike until Jim Lorentz swatted him into oblivion, and then an eerie, dense fog formed over the ice surface due to unseasonably warm May temperatures in Buffalo. It was one of the strangest and most memorable nights in Sabres history, and in the end it also became one of the happiest – though not for the bat – when Rene Robert scored in overtime to win Game 3 of the 1975 Stanley Cup Finals against Philadelphia.

During Game 1 of the 1975 Stanley Cup Finals in the Philadelphia Spectrum, a witty and – as it turned out – prophetic Flyers fan hung a banner that read: "Jesus Saves – But Nobody Saves More Than Parent."

The reference was to Flyers goaltender Bernie Parent, one of the best netminders in NHL history who was fresh off leading the Flyers to the NHL championship in 1974, and was enjoying a marvelous run through the '75 playoffs.

No one had to remind the Buffalo Sabres of Parent's brilliance because entering the Finals, they hadn't beaten Bernie in their last 14 games spanning his original stint with Philadelphia, a brief stopover in Toronto, and then again when he returned to the Flyers.

"I see him in my soup every day," Buffalo right wing Rene Robert once said. "Bernie Parent was probably the finest goalie I ever faced."

After stretching their futility streak against Parent to 16 by losing the first two games of the Finals in Philadelphia, and scoring just two goals in the process, it was quite apparent the Sabres were going to need some help if they were going to defeat Parent and the Broad Street Bullies. It didn't figure that fog would turn out to be Buffalo's saving grace, but hey, you take what you can get when you're facing someone who saves more than Jesus.

When the Sabres returned home to Memorial Auditorium for Game 3, they found their old barn in disarray. Thanks to unseasonably hot and muggy 90-degree weather, the Aud was transformed into the world's largest sauna. With no air conditioning to keep the building cool, the temperature outside turned the ice to mush and by the third period an eerie fog began to hover over the playing surface.

Persevering through the bizarre playing conditions, defenseman Bill Hajt scored with about 10 minutes remaining in regulation to tie the game for Buffalo, and then 18:29 into overtime Robert scored the winner, bringing to an end one of the most memorable nights in the Aud's long, proud history.

"It was like playing in a graveyard," said Sabres defenseman Jerry Korab of the fog. And no doubt the building – packed to the rafters with 15,863 rabid Sabres fans –

would have been quiet as a graveyard had Philadelphia won. Instead, Robert's goal – fired from a bad angle, a shot Parent probably would have stopped with ease had he been able to see it – lifted the Sabres back into the series, at least momentarily.

"We had to win this one," said Buffalo's Jim Lorentz, who played a central role in another of this night's dramas – the slaying of the bat. Early in the game a bat got loose and was flying around pestering the fans and players. Finally during a stoppage in play, Lorentz managed to whack the bat with his stick, killing it. It drew a huge cheer from the fans and also inflated Lorentz's mail bag.

"Everyone was looking at each other because no one wanted to pick it up," Lorentz recalled. "Finally Rick MacLeish took his glove off and carried it to the penalty box. Afterwards I got letters from all over the country including a little old lady from Maine criticizing me for killing a helpless bat."

The night began with the fans giving their Sabres a thunderous two-minute standing ovation when they skated onto the ice. "Standing there before the first game of the Finals at the Aud was amazing," Korab recalled. "The place was just shaking."

Once the game began, it was Buffalo goalie Gerry Desjardins who was shaking. For some reason the veteran was unusually nervous and unable to get himself mentally into the game. Thirty-nine seconds in Gary Dornhoefer scored, and at 3:09 Desjardins whiffed on Don Saleski's slap shot from the blue line and it was 2-0. So much for an early jolt of adrenaline.

Goals by Danny Gare and Rick Martin 17 seconds apart pulled Buffalo even and proved that Parent was human, but MacLeish beat Desjardins with another long shot to give the Flyers the lead at the end of the first period. To his credit Desjardins realized it wasn't his night and he asked coach Floyd Smith to take him out and insert Roger Crozier. Smith agreed, and Crozier allowed just one goal over the final 58:29.

"After the second goal against

(Buffalo Sabres)

Danny Gare scored a goal 18 seconds into his first game in the NHL, and when the Sabres went to the Stanley Cup Finals in that 1974-75 season, Gare chipped in 31 goals and 31 assists.

me I thought it was a grand time to get the hell out of there," Desjardins said. "I asked to leave at the end of the period. I knew if I stayed in everything would have gone down the drain. After all, we were only down one goal. The guys were working so hard, they could win the game, so why not put in Roger? I couldn't stop a football, I was a second slow on every shot."

Don Luce and Philadelphia's Reg Leach traded second-period goals, and then Hajt swatted in a rebound after Parent had stopped Martin to tie the game at 4-4. It was about this time that the fog rolled in, and during the third period the game was halted 12 times so that the players could skate circles around the ice in an effort to dissipate the soupy mist.

DANNY GARE

He made his NHL debut on opening night of the 1974-75 season in Boston against the Bruins, and it took all of 18 seconds for Gare to announce his arrival as he scored on his very first NHL shift.

"That was very exciting for me," Gare said of coach Floyd Smith's decision to start the game with the line of Gare, Don Luce and Craig Ramsay on the ice. "The Bruins had played the Flyers in the Stanley Cup Finals the previous spring and here I was facing off against Esposito, Hodge, Cashman, Orr and Vadnais. The puck went around the boards, Schony took a shot and I got the rebound."

From that moment on, Gare – Buffalo's second-round choice in the 1974 NHL Entry Draft – was considered a goal scorer, and rarely did he disappoint.

By the end of his rookie season he had 31 goals and the Sabres were playing for the Stanley Cup, though they lost to Philadelphia. His sophomore year he erupted for 50, and in 1979-80, Scotty Bowman's first Buffalo team, Gare scored a team-record 56, a mark that stood until Alexander Mogilny scored 76 in 1992-93.

One of the most beloved players in franchise history because not only was he a goal scorer, he was a small, feisty winger who wasn't afraid to plaster an opponent with a check or drop the gloves, Gare ranks fourth all-time for Buffalo in goals with 267.

Where he does not rank very high is in games played because in 1981, Bowman included Gare, Jim Schoenfeld and Derek Smith in a trade with Detroit for Mike Foligno, Dale McCourt and Brent Peterson, one of the biggest in team history. "He was looking to improve the team by getting some younger players and I can understand his side of it, but it was very difficult for me," Gare said.

He played 4 1/2 years with the Red Wings and one last season with Wayne Gretzky in Edmonton in 1986-87 before retiring. After a stint in the front office of the Tampa Bay Lightning, Gare has been back in Buffalo for nearly a decade as a member of the Sabres' broadcast team for the Empire Sports Network.

"It got so bad that I couldn't see the puck when it was 10 feet inside the blue line," said Parent. "I wished I had radar on my nose."

Despite both goalies having to play virtually blindfolded, neither team scored in the final 10 minutes of regulation, nor in the first 18 minutes of the overtime. But then the French Connection – defused for the previous seven playoff games as they'd scored only one goal – ignited.

Martin gathered a loose puck off the boards and passed ahead to Gilbert Perreault in the neutral zone. The slick centerman skated across the red line and fired the puck into the corner to Parent's left. Robert zipped past Flyers defenseman Jimmy Watson and as the puck bounced back toward the faceoff circle Robert whipped a shot on net. Parent couldn't see and it skidded between his legs and into the mesh, setting off a raucous celebration.

"Rene yelled to me and I saw him going to the corner," said Perreault. "I was in the middle about five feet inside the red line, so I passed to the boards in the corner."

Robert then picked up the commentary. "It's almost impossible to score from that

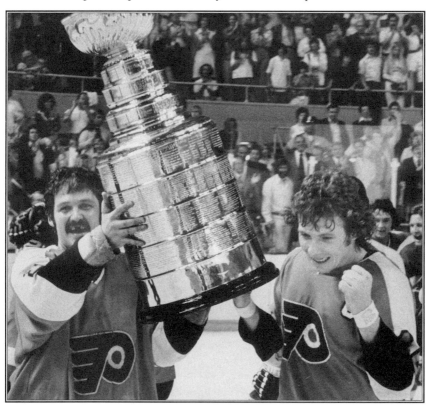

(Buffalo Sabres)

Buffalo might have won the Stanley Cup in 1975 had it not been for the remarkable play in net of Philadelphia goalie Bernie Parent (left), who paraded the coveted chalice around the Memorial Auditorium ice along with Flyers captain Bobby Clarke.

angle, but I shot at the net hoping somebody could get the rebound. It seemed to me (Parent) wasn't ready for the shot."

Parent said he was ready, he just couldn't see. "I didn't see Perreault's pass, and I saw Robert's shot too late for me to come out and stop it."

This was Buffalo's fifth overtime playoff game in its history, and for the third time, it was Robert who scored the winner. But he admitted this one was a bit tainted. "From where I scored that goal you could probably shoot 100 pucks and never score," he said. "I was just trying to put the puck on net."

Luckily that puck found the net, and Buffalo rode that surge of momentum two nights later when it scored three third-period goals to pull out a series-tying 4-2 victory in Game 4. However, the Sabres' couldn't snap their Spectrum jinx and lost Game 5 in Philadelphia, then were stoned by Parent in Game 6 back at the Aud as the goalie pitched a 2-0 shutout and the Flyers carried the Stanley Cup around for all of Buffalo to see. Parent won the Conn Smythe Trophy as playoff MVP thanks to his 1.88 goals-against average. "I thought we certainly had the better team, but the major point was the play of Bernie Parent," said Lorentz.
"He was on another planet."

April 17, 1979 – Buffalo, N.Y.
War Memorial Stadium

Welcome Back, Baseball

Baseball made a triumphant return to Buffalo in 1979 after a nearly nine-year absence, and while the city didn't warm immediately to the Double-A brand of the grand game, it wasn't long before this Pittsburgh Pirates' farm club began winning the fans over with their penchant for hitting home runs and bantering with the customers at War Memorial Stadium. After three days of weather-induced postponements, the new Bisons finally took the field, and they went out and won their opener on Luis Salazar's dramatic three-run homer in the bottom of the ninth inning.

Throughout the 1960s the Buffalo Bisons cringed every time they walked into decrepit War Memorial Stadium. And it was their home park, so you can imagine what the visiting teams must have felt like having to play there.

They called the place the Rockpile because, well, it was literally becoming a rock pile, crumbling all around them just like the east-side neighborhood where it was located. Truer words were never spoken than in 1967 when Bob Howsam, president of the parent club Cincinnati Reds, said upon discontinuing the team's affiliation with Buffalo, "War Memorial Stadium is no place to develop young ballplayers."

Even before Howsam's comment, Buffalonians had decreed that War Memorial Stadium was no place to go watch a baseball game, either. And when attendance hit rock bottom early in 1970, the International League voted in favor of allowing Buffalo's new parent club, Montreal, to move the Triple-A team to Winnipeg, leaving the city without professional baseball for the first time since 1876.

It's funny how one man's cave can be another man's castle, and how absence really does make the heart grow fonder.

When the Bisons were reborn in 1979 in the form of an Eastern League Double-A team, the new crop of players fell in love with their old new home. And as for the fans, they weren't particularly thrilled with Double-A baseball given their major league status with the Bills and Sabres, but at least it was baseball, professional baseball, something they had lacked for nearly nine years.

"The parks we played in at Single-A were glorified high school fields, and then all of a sudden we get called up to Buffalo in 1979 and we walk into this stadium and it was incredible," remembered outfielder Rick Lancellotti who became an instant hero that year when he cracked 41 home runs to tie a league record.

"We were so used to playing on these small fields, it was such a blast to be in that stadium. As rickety as it was, as old as it was, it was kind of cool. Just to hear the ball come off the bat in a stadium as opposed to an open field was different. I loved it."

So did the fans.

"Baseball belongs in Buffalo," said Mayor Jimmy Griffin, the No. 1 fan who was instrumental in reviving the sport in the city and was on hand to throw out the ceremonial first pitch at the freshly painted ballpark.

So it was that when hizzoner, the liberal left-hander from South Buffalo, winged the ball toward home plate – Bob Uecker would have said "just a bit outside" – baseball was back in Buffalo. And while Opening Day had been delayed three days because of snow and rain, it didn't seem like much of a wait in the wake of a nine-year baseball drought for the 2,132 fans who braved temperatures in the 30s to witness the game's return.

For the record, the new Bisons – farmhands of the Pittsburgh Pirates – were 3-0 winners in their first game, pulling out the victory in dramatic fashion. With the game scoreless in the bottom of the ninth, Lancellotti stroked a two-out single, Tony Pena reached base on an error by Reading shortstop Pete Dempsey, and both trotted home triumphantly when Luis Salazar delivered a titanic game-winning three-run homer to right-center on a 3-2 pitch.

"What a great way to win a ballgame," the mayor proclaimed. "A home run with two outs in the last of the ninth. What can you say? I was jumping up and down and cheering like everyone else."

Never mind that the Phillies came back to win the nightcap 11-8 despite more Bison butane when Lancellotti hit a two-out, two-run homer that tied the game and forced extra innings. This was one of the grand days in Buffalo's near century-old baseball history.

"I remember we won the opener," Lancellotti said. "It was so great to just walk out there and be part of it. And it made the feeling even greater because we knew the people had been without baseball for a long time. There were a lot of people there, and

(Buffalo Bisons)

War Memorial Stadium, shown here in 1960, became the home of the Bisons when baseball returned to Buffalo after a nine-year absence in 1979. Rick Lancellotti took advantage of the short porch in right field to hit 41 home runs that year.

to get them to come down on a cold April day was fun."

Fun would be one way to describe the season Lancellotti had in Buffalo. The fence was only 289 feet down the right-field line, and for the lefty-swinging Lancellotti, it was home run heaven, though not right away.

"The thing about playing with a short porch, you have a tendency to hit everything up and I found that out," said Lancellotti, whose 41 homers rank third all-time in Bison land behind Ollie Carnegie (45 in 1938) and Bill Kelly (44 in 1926). "I only had a few home runs by early May and they were thinking about sending me down.

Everything was going wrong, so I had a meeting with Steve (Demeter, a member of the 1955 Bisons who was the club's manager) and I begged him to hit me fourth. He had me down at eight and I felt useless down there. He said 'Why should I hit you fourth, you're not hitting?' So back and forth we went, but he put me at cleanup."

That move woke Lancellotti's bat and he began sending lasers into the seats, one coming in mid-June when a crowd of 13,422 gathered at the stadium to watch a doubleheader against West Haven, the New York Yankees' affiliate. That day, a kid named Buck Showalter homered for West Haven to help his club gain a split.

Lancellotti, who finished with a team-high 107 RBI while batting .287, wasn't the only masher in the lineup. Pena – who would go on to become the most productive major leaguer from that Buffalo team as he spent parts of 18 seasons with six teams, most prominently Pittsburgh, St. Louis and Boston – ripped 34 homers, drove in 97 runs, hit .313 and was a dazzling fielding catcher. Salazar batted .323 with 27 dingers, and as a team the Bisons set an Eastern League record with 199 homers. Amazingly, Lancellotti, Pena and Salazar were Demeter's 7-8-9 hitters in the Opening Day lineup.

"We used to give up some runs, but we'd rack up a bunch, too," said Lancellotti, who married a Buffalo girl, the former Debbie Ludtka, and made his home in Buffalo after his retirement from pro baseball in 1992. Today he runs his own business, the Buffalo School of Baseball, where he teaches boys and girls the art of hitting a baseball.

Lancellotti was just a young pup of 22 when he played in Buffalo in 1979. He went on to become the ultimate baseball gypsy and became known as the real-life Crash Davis – Davis being the fictional character played by Kevin Costner in the 1988 movie *Bull Durham*. Davis was a slugging catcher who bounced around the minors smashing home runs and offering savvy and stability to young ballclubs, only to be bypassed for major league jobs by many of the youngsters he cajoled and counseled.

That's Lancellotti. In addition to the Eastern League, Lancellotti also led the Pacific Coast League, the International League, and the Japanese League in home runs, and he won his titles in three different decades. During his baseball odyssey he played for about 15 teams in seven countries and on four continents. In all he hit 276 minor-league home runs which very well could be a record, plus another 58 during his two years in Japan. But Lancellotti never was given a realistic chance to play in the majors. He had cups of coffee with San Diego (1982), San Francisco (1986) and Boston (1990), but he had only 58 at-bats and two homers, both with the Giants.

"That's what lets me sleep at night," Lancellotti said of the two homers he hit in the majors. "After putting up that many years and those kind of numbers, I wish things could have turned out differently, but at least I got there. There's some sanity there that I can live with. When you're playing ball, they tell you you need to hit 20 homers, then

---

TONY PENA

While Rick Lancellotti was wowing fans in 1979 with a left-handed home run stroke that was tailor-made for War Memorial Stadium, the player that captured the fans' hearts was Pena, an Energizer bunny of a catcher who never stopped talking and never stopped hustling.

"The people will call to me on the field and I answer them," Pena said during his lone season in Buffalo. "I want the people to know what kind of player I am. I love the people in Buffalo. To me they're like my friends and I want to play hard for them."

And he did. On the last day of the 1979 season, Pena slammed three home runs and Buffalo defeated Reading, costing the Phillies a spot in the Eastern League playoffs. "This was my goodbye to Buffalo," said the Dominican-born Pena, who knew, like everyone else, that he wouldn't be back in Double-A the following year. "This is the first town I played in in the United States where people loved the game. I will remember Buffalo for the rest of my life."

Pena was a terrific catcher in the minors. He had a flashy receiving style and a powerful arm, and he only improved once he made it to the big leagues with Pittsburgh in 1980. He won four National League gold gloves and played in five All-Star games, mostly due to his defensive wizardry because he was only a .260 hitter with 107 career home runs.

During his one year in Buffalo, though, Pena was a hitting machine. He batted .313 and those last three homers against Reading gave him 34 for the year, second only to Lancellotti's 41.

"Tony just happened to be one of those guys who was extreme hustle to the max which you never saw in catchers," Lancellotti said. "Usually catchers don't outrun guys to first base or throw the ball back to the pitcher harder than the pitcher threw it in the first place. You knew only good things were going to happen for him. He could do it all."

---

you hit 30 and you don't move. After a while, little by little it breaks you down."

Lancellotti only recently began embracing the comparison to the fictional Crash Davis. "Actually all it reminded me of was how long I played, and it really wasn't that big of an honor, but as I get older and I realize I hit 276 home runs in the minor leagues I thought 'OK, at least I did something, I have something to be proud of.' At the time you're doing it, you're not that proud of it. You don't sit back and say 'Wow, what a great year' because if you're not going up to the majors, you're not looking at it that way. Now you look back and you think it's kind of neat."

No one knew who Lancellotti was on Opening Day. For that matter, no one knew who any of these guys were. But before long, the fans and the team meshed.

The first-game starter, Fred Breining, struck out the first six batters he faced and retired the first nine. A perfect game on the first Opening Day in nine years? Well, no. Jay Loviglio led off the fourth with a single to ruin that improbable storyline. Still, Breining was brilliant. He threw a complete game three-hitter with 14 strikeouts.

"My forkball was working exceptionally well," he said. "It was one of the best games I ever pitched. I thought I would just go seven innings, but after I did (Demeter) asked me how I felt and I said I wanted the win."

Thanks to Salazar, he got it. Reading starter Scott Munninghoff handcuffed the Bisons on one hit – a single by Pena in the fifth – before departing after the sixth in favor of Don Fowler. Fowler continued the Phillies' mastery as he worked two hitless innings, but after Lancellotti's single and Dempsey's error which allowed Pena to reach, Fowler seemed rattled and he made a big mistake with Salazar at the plate.

"The first pitcher was throwing me low," said Salazar, who struck out his three previous at-bats. "(Fowler) threw me a high, outside slider and I was just trying to make contact and go to right field. I knew it was gone when I hit it."

And while it wasn't 75,000 people at Rich Stadium, or 18,000 at HSBC Arena or 21,000 at Dunn Tire Park, those 2,132 in attendance – baseball fanatics who had longed for this day for nine years – went crazy.

"The fans seemed to have liked what they saw and I think they'll be back," Demeter said.

A total of 133,418 paying customers showed up at the stadium that year, a league-leading total, proving that baseball could work in Buffalo. In 1984, the last year of the Double-A Bisons, 223,443 came to the park to watch a team that finished just five games over .500. Once the Bisons graduated back to Triple-A in 1985 when they joined the American Association, baseball was truly entrenched once again. Nearly a half million fans watched the 1987 team close out War Memorial Stadium once and for all, and when Pilot Field opened for business in 1988, the Bisons shattered minor-league baseball attendance records. The 1991 gate of 1,240,951 is still the highest single-season mark in minor league history. As for the prominent players on that 1979 team, Pena was a career .260 hitter who played in five All-Star games, won four National League gold glove awards, and is now the manager of the Kansas City Royals. Salazar played parts of 13 major league seasons mostly with San Diego, the White Sox and the Cubs, and was a .261 career hitter. He appeared in the 1984 World Series for the Padres. Pitcher Dave Dravecky went 64-57 with a 3.59 ERA in eight seasons with San Diego and San Francisco before surgery to remove a cancerous tumor from his arm ended his career in 1989. Breining pitched four years with his hometown San Francisco Giants and posted a 27-20 record with a 3.34 ERA.

September 7, 1980 – Orchard Park, N.Y.
Rich Stadium

The End of the Miami Jinx

No Bills' fan will ever forget it. For the entire decade of the 1970s the Bills lost every game they played against Miami, an NFL-record streak of 20 consecutive losses by one team to another. So when the streak finally came to an end on opening day of the 1980 season, the Bills and their fans acted like they had just won the Super Bowl.

Offensive guard Bob Kuechenberg never thought he'd see the day when his Miami Dolphins would lose to the Buffalo Bills.

It was incomprehensible, and he said so during the 1974 season: "Buffalo will never beat Miami as long as I am playing," Kuechenberg said.

Kuechenberg had joined the Dolphins in 1970 and that year, Miami whipped the Bills twice, 33-14 and 45-7. By the time he made his bold statement, the Dolphins – coming off back-to-back Super Bowl triumphs – were 8-0 against Buffalo with Kuechenberg sporting his familiar No. 67 jersey.

Through the years, the Bills scared the Dolphins on a few occasions, but Don Shula's troops always found a way to win. And when the 1979 season – Kuechenberg's 10th in the NFL – came to a close, he still hadn't suffered the ignominy of losing to the Bills.

As the Dolphins rode into Rich Stadium for the 1980 season opener against Buffalo, Miami had beaten the Bills 20 straight times, an NFL record for a winning streak by one team over another that neatly encompassed the entire decade of the 1970s.

Kuechenberg had considered retiring before the 1980 campaign began, and as it turned out, perhaps he should have because on a gloriously sunny day in the suburbs of Buffalo, the unthinkable happened: The goal posts came tumbling down as the Bills ended their agonizing drought with a 17-7 victory over the Dolphins.

"Yeah, I said that," Kuechenberg replied when asked about his comment in 1974. "But it's obvious that it's all over now. Maybe I shouldn't have come back from retirement."

For three and a half quarters, it was the kind of game that had come to define Buffalo's struggles against Miami. The Bills played sloppily, and tried their hardest to give the Dolphins a victory. Bills quarterback Joe Ferguson threw five interceptions, Buffalo lost two fumbles, and a blocked punt in the third quarter had allowed Miami to take a 7-3 lead.

"I admit I thought `Here we go again' after they scored early in the third to go ahead 7-3," said Ferguson, 0-14 against Miami entering the day.

But instead of drooping his head as Ferguson was known to do during his 12 years in Buffalo, he fought back gamely and produced two touchdowns in the final four minutes as Miami – not the Bills – made the crucial mistakes down the stretch.

"I'm proud of Joe Ferguson," said guard Reggie McKenzie, who had endured 16 straight losses to Miami. "He hung in there today. He was really PO'ed, but he hung in there."

Both teams started poorly as they combined for six turnovers in the first 20 minutes, but that sixth, a diving interception by Buffalo's Jeff Nixon at the Miami 32 midway through the second quarter set up Nick Mike-Mayer's 40-yard field goal to give the Bills a 3-0 lead.

The Bills drove to the Miami 27 at the end of the half, but a series of miscues short-circuited the promising march and Ferguson's pass toward the end zone on the final play before intermission was intercepted by Gerald Small.

Buffalo was stopped on its first possession of the third quarter and when long snapper Chris Keating sent a one-hopper back to punter Greg Cater, Kim Bokamper was able to slice through and partially block Cater's kick. Miami took over at the Bills 27 and scored four plays later as Steve Howell broke a 17-yard run to set up Bob Griese's four-yard TD pass to Tony Nathan.

Ferguson was intercepted twice more before the third quarter ended, and on Buffalo's first possession of the fourth period, he suffered his fifth pick as safety Glenn Blackwood stepped in front of a pass intended for Jerry Butler at the Miami 29.

That one was particularly painful because the Bills had gambled a few plays earlier when notoriously conservative Buffalo coach Chuck Knox called for a fake punt from the 50. Cater pulled it off, throwing a 15-yard pass to tight end Mark Brammer, and with the crowd of nearly 80,000 in a frenzy, the Bills appeared to have the momentum needed to pull off the upset.

"That play really got us pumped up," said Ferguson. "I was on the sideline thinking `What's going on here?' That was a big play no matter what happened (immediately after)."

Undaunted by the futility of the offense, the Bills' defense continued to play heroically, keeping Buffalo within striking distance.

"That's how every game should be played," said defensive tackle Mike Kadish of Buffalo's defensive intensity. "We fought through so much adversity, but we never gave up. This is probably the best defensive effort since I've been here."

Despite the solid defense, the Bills were still trailing when they took possession at their own 32 with 6:44 left to play. Time was running out, and Ferguson knew he had to make something happen.

After making two first downs, Ferguson executed a crucial play, hitting Butler on a deep out for a 29-yard gain to the 11 with 3:56 left.

"We were in a zone and I had deep coverage," said Blackwood. "I was looking for help outside, that's where you get it. He just broke out. I should have been there. That one really hurt."

An offsides penalty on the Dolphins moved the ball to the 6, and Curtis Brown gained two off the right side. Ferguson then rolled to his left and fired a dangerous pass to the left front corner of the end zone to fullback Roosevelt Leaks. Leaks made the catch in heavy traffic and crashed over the goal line with 3:42 remaining to give the Bills a 10-7 lead.

"If anybody was responsible for picking up Leaks, it would be me," said Miami safety Tim Foley. "Sometimes it's hard to see what's happening from back there. I guess I was turned too inside to get wide fast enough."

When the Miami offense took the field after the kickoff, Don Strock, not Griese, led them out. Shula was opting for Strock's stronger arm and greater mobility, but the move backfired on Strock's third play when he tried to throw down the middle and was intercepted by linebacker Isiah Robertson.

With the deafening roar of the crowd virtually carrying him through the Dolphins like a hot dog wrapper in a hurricane, Robertson weaved his way 39 yards to the 11. And on fourth-and-one from the two, Joe Cribbs leaped over the top for the game-clinching touchdown, setting off a celebration the likes of which Buffalonians hadn't participated in since 1964 when the Jack Kemp-led Bills won their first AFL

(Courier-Express)

The Bills snapped their NFL record losing streak to Miami at 20 games with a 17-7 victory in September 1980 at Rich Stadium, and the fans celebrated the historic day by storming the field and tearing down the goal posts.

Championship at old War Memorial Stadium.

"We were in deep trouble when they scored (for the 10-7 lead)," Kuechenberg said. "Still, there was room for a miracle. But when Isiah Robertson picked up the interception on our next series, the party was over."

Said Knox: "It was a great win by a bunch of guys who were not going to be denied. I don't think I've ever seen a football team that came any more ready to play. In my 27 years of coaching, I've never seen such determination."

Bills owner Ralph Wilson called it "the biggest win we've ever had here in 20

(Courier-Express)

In his first game as a member of the Bills, Joe Cribbs rushed for 60 yards and scoring the clinching touchdown in the fourth quarter to help the Bills end their dreaded jinx against Miami.

years." He also said he would gladly foot the bill for two new goal posts.

"They brought the one goal post up to me," Wilson said. "They carried it up the whole stadium, but they couldn't get it in the box because it was too long. That was a

---

JERRY BUTLER

It wasn't so much Jerry Butler's skill that impressed his former Bills' teammate, Fred Smerlas, as much as it was the effortless way he put that skill to work.

"I never knew what soft hands were until the first time I saw Jerry catch a football when we were rookies in 1979," Smerlas said. "With most receivers, even some of the better ones in the game, you hear at least a small pop when ball meets flesh. With Jerry, the only sound you heard was pooofff. It was as if the ball landed on a bed of feathers. I can honestly say I've never heard that sound with any other pass catcher.

"Jerry Butler was one of the greatest athletes I ever saw. He had no fear when it came to catching the football and that probably contributed to his injuries. It's too bad he didn't remain healthy because he could have rewritten some records."

Butler was the Bills' first-round draft choice in 1979, and four games into his first NFL season Buffalo fans knew this was a special player. In a game against the New York Jets at Rich Stadium, Butler caught 10 passes for 255 yards and four touchdowns.

"That stands as the pinnacle for me," Butler said of that afternoon. "It was the kind of day that every receiver dreams about, but few have the luck to experience."

Unfortunately, Butler was felled by a pair of serious injuries – a torn-up knee in 1983 and a broken leg which ended his career midway through 1986, far too soon. Butler caught 278 passes for 4,301 yards and 29 TDs during the 5 1/2 years he was able to play.

"If those injuries had not occurred, Butler could have become a great one," said former Miami coach Don Shula.

---

great day, one that I'll never forget."

Nose tackle Fred Smerlas had only been a part of the last two losses in the streak, but he knew what the Miami game meant to the organization and the fans.

"I remember the spirit going into that game," Smerlas said. "We walked onto that field and it was like a new era had begun. The fans were pumped, Chuck's boys were tough, and there was no question, no reservation in anyone's heart that we were going to win that game. It was an electric atmosphere. When that final gun sounded and we beat them, there were no problems in the world that day. It was unbelievable."

After the game, players and fans partied together on the field. One of the newest Bills – veteran guard Conrad Dobler – was awestruck by the fans' emotion. "It was like a rock concert, and we were like Mick Jagger and the Rolling Stones," Dobler said.

"Some fans even handed out beers to the players still on the field. I got one, and so did by buddy, Phil Villapiano. `This is our kind of town,' we said to each other, clinking beer cups as we made our way to the dressing room."

As Kuechenberg sat in the cramped visitors locker room at Rich, he rightfully praised the Bills for a job well done.

"The difference was the Bills didn't beat themselves, we beat ourselves," he said. "We made the big plays in the fourth quarter over the course of the last 10 years. That's how we managed to put together a 20-game winning streak against Buffalo. The streak against Buffalo is something I will stand back on 20 years from now and be proud of. It had to end sometime."

He then summed up the feelings of Bills fans everywhere when he said: "A lot of Bills fans felt like they were 0-20. It was something for the city to enjoy. If the shoe were on the other foot, I'd call for work, school and everything else to be closed tomorrow. The fans endured and they deserve a holiday."

That victory began one of the most memorable seasons in Bills history. The Talkin' Proud Bills won their first five games and eventually finished 11-5, winning their first AFC East division title on the last day of the season when they survived a tough game in San Francisco against young Joe Montana and the soon-to-be dynastic 49ers. However, with Ferguson limping on a badly sprained ankle, Buffalo lost to San Diego, 20-14, in the divisional playoffs on Dan Fouts' TD pass to Ron Smith with less than two minutes to play. Miami never seemed to shake the shock of losing to Buffalo and wound up 8-8 and missed the playoffs.

September 4, 1990 – Buffalo, N.Y.
Pilot Field

18 Innings

Buffalo manager Terry Collins said it best when he opined that "If that was a major league game, it would be on Classic Sports all the time." He's right. Apparently it wasn't dramatic enough that Buffalo and Nashville needed a special one-game play-off to decide the American Association's Eastern Division title, so the two teams played 18 tension-filled innings before the Sounds emerged victorious in front of a wide-eyed turned sleepy-eyed crowd at Pilot Field.

Just before the start of the one-game playoff that would decide the American Association's Eastern Division championship, Buffalo Bisons pitching coach Jackie Brown strolled over to Nashville manager Pete Mackanin to say a quick hello, and to turn the screws a few grooves.

The previous winter Mackanin's Venezuelan Winter League team had lost to Buffalo manager Terry Collins' club in a similar one-game playoff to determine who would earn the fourth and final berth in the postseason. On that South American night, Collins' team prevailed in a 14-inning marathon, and Brown couldn't resist reminding Mackanin.

"If you can believe this, Jackie told me we'd probably end up playing until four in the morning and we'd end up flipping a coin to see who wins," Mackanin said.

The Bisons and Sounds didn't need a coin to decide the issue, but they did need 18 innings, which translated into more than five hours of some of the highest drama in Buffalo baseball history, before Mackinin earned the sweetest of revenge when Nashville pulled out a 4-3 victory.

"I thought about that all game," Mackanin said of Brown's pre-game tease. "I thought 'If Terry beats me here, I'm going to have a complex.'"

Instead, when Chris Jones lined an RBI double off Buffalo's Blas Minor – just called up from Double-A Harrisburg earlier that day – the Sounds had their first division title since joining the triple-A American Association in 1985. In the process they extended the Bisons' drought of not having won a division championship since 1959 when they played in the International League.

"This game right here, this is one you can write about for a month," Buffalo first baseman Mark Ryal said to a group of reporters. That seemed about right, seeing that it took almost that long for the game to be played.

Yet while the end result created an atmosphere inside the Buffalo clubhouse usually reserved for wakes, and it sent 16,224 fans home with frowns on their sleepy faces, every tension-packed minute had been worth it.

That night Collins had said through glassy eyes that "In 20 years there never has been a game I wanted to win more. It's a crushing blow." Nearly a decade later during a visit to Buffalo for an old-timers game, proving that time does indeed heal all wounds, Collins recognized that the game had been one of those epochal events that every player and manager dreams to be a part of, win or lose.

"If that was a major league game, it would be on Classic Sports all the time," Collins said.

Well, the hell with ESPN Classic. If they don't want to relive it, we will.

The Bisons had a chance to wrap up the division on the last night of the regular season, but they lost 8-1 in Indianapolis while Nashville was rallying for four runs in the eighth inning to defeat Louisville, creating a tie for the top spot, each team with 85-61 records. Because Buffalo had won 11 of 18 games against Nashville that year, the tiebreaker was played at Buffalo's sparkling three-year-old downtown ballpark, then known as Pilot Field.

When the Bisons emerged from the dugout they were greeted by a standing ovation, and Collins remembered looking into the stands and being awestruck by the size of the crowd because the club barely had time to print tickets let alone sell them for the impromptu game. "To sell that many tickets was pretty stinking impressive," Collins said. "Both teams walked out on the field and said, 'Holy cow, this means a lot.'"

Buffalo was fortunate that it was Dorn Taylor's turn to pitch in the rotation. Taylor had compiled a 14-7 record in 1990, and more impressively, during his Bison career he was 21-7 with a 1.59 ERA in games at Pilot Field. So when the Bisons opened a quick 2-0 lead on Ryal's two-out, first-inning double to left-center that scored John Cangelosi, and shortstop Carlos Garcia's home run in the second, they couldn't help but feel that this was going to be their night. "He was the most consistent pitcher in the league at that time," said Garcia. "He was the best one we had on that team, the one guy we wanted."

However, Buffalo's season-long bugaboo – poor fielding – contributed to the surrendering of that lead in the next two innings. In the third Nashville's Freddie Benavides led off with a single and Skeeter Barnes executed a perfect hit-and-run with a single to right. Buffalo right fielder Ty Gainey came up throwing in an attempt to nail Benavides at third, but he misfired badly and Benavides was able to trot home.

Taylor escaped without further damage, but another error cost him in the fourth. Keith Lockhart opened with a single and took second when Leo Garcia grounded out to first. Taylor recorded a strikeout for the second out, but with Benavides at the plate, Taylor bounced a wild pitch in front of catcher Tom Prince. Prince blocked the ball and it squirted about 10 feet to his right, which turned out to be a bad break because after he retrieved it, he tried to gun down the advancing Lockhart. His throw sailed into left field and Lockhart scrambled home with the tying run.

The game remained tied as Buffalo blew a great opportunity in the bottom of the seventh when Cangelosi grounded out with the bases loaded. In the eighth, with Taylor gone in favor of a pinch-hitter and Miguel Garcia on the mound for Buffalo, Jones, just inserted as a pinch-hitter, whacked Garcia's second pitch far over the left-field fence to give the Sounds a 3-2 lead.

Urged on by the big crowd, the Bisons responded in the bottom of the eighth. Kevin Burdick led off with a walk and was replaced by pinch-runner Jeff Richardson. Steve Carter, after twice failing to get a sacrifice bunt down, singled to left, and then Ryal moved the runners along with a sacrifice bringing Orlando Merced to the plate. With first base open, Mackanin decided to go after Merced, and the Sounds retired him, but his grounder scored Richardson with the tying run. With a chance to drive in the go-

(Buffalo Bisons)

The 1990 American Association Eastern Division pennant race was decided in a special one-game playoff at Buffalo's Pilot Field, and the Bisons' exhausted and dejected dugout tells the story of what happened. Nashville outlasted Buffalo 4-3 in an 18-inning marathon.

ahead run, Prince struck out leaving men stranded at the corners.

It would be nearly three hours before another run would score, though not for a lack of trying.

Errors by Merced and Garcia helped Nashville load the bases in the ninth, but Barnes lined into an inning-ending double play, and when the Bisons stranded Richardson at second in their half, the game entered extra innings. Incredibly, the night was only half over.

Buffalo loaded the bases in the 10th, Nashville did it in the 11th, and then the Bisons did it again in the bottom of the 11th and very nearly ended the game. Cangelosi, the fastest Bison, was on third when Danny Sheaffer hit a shallow fly ball to center. Collins knew it would be a gamble because the ball wasn't hit that well, but with the division title on the line he decided to send Cangelosi.

"In a game like this you never know when you're going to get another opportunity to score," Cangelosi said. "We wanted to be the aggressor. We wanted him to have to make a great throw."

Nashville's Leo Garcia did. He threw a perfect strike to catcher Tony DeFrancesco who applied the tag while being bowled over by Cangelosi. "He was our best base runner," Collins said of Cangelosi. "I thought that fly ball was deep enough and Leo just made a great throw. You tip your hat."

For the third inning in a row the Bisons loaded the bases in the 12th, and this time Cangelosi killed the threat by grounding out on the first pitch he saw. In the 15th Buffalo reliever Roger Mason escaped a bases-loaded quandary, and then in the bottom half the Bisons put runners on the corners only to see pitcher Rick Reed – pinch-hitting because Collins was out of position players – strike out.

"At one point, I was ticked off, at another point I was subdued, and then I was ticked off again," Mackanin said. "I finally said, 'This is totally absurd. It's out of my hands.'"

Said Collins: "The biggest thing I remember is all the opportunities we had. We couldn't score."

Then again, neither could Nashville. After Miguel Garcia had allowed Jones' homer in the eighth, relievers Mark Huismann, Mark Ross, Mason and Minor had been fabulous, giving up just five hits in nine innings. "I thought it was going to be over so many times," said Mason. "You'd get so fired up and think it would end, then have to go out and pitch again. That was the toughest part."

No, the toughest part is what happened in the 18th inning.

With Minor – who didn't even know most of his teammates' names – into his third inning of work, Billy Bates singled with one out, took second on a groundout, and chugged home when Jones pulled a fastball down the third-base line past Tommy Shields for a double.

"Unfortunately I got a pitch up in the strike zone," said Minor. "We knew he was a fastball hitter so I threw a split-finger but got it up."

Minor, who would go on to play a key role on Buffalo's 1991 division-winning club, recalled the feeling of joining the team that day and then being thrust into such a volatile situation that night – or, in reality, that next morning.

"I was surprised I was put in when I was," he said. "Initially I was real nervous, but after watching the game for 15 innings things started to level off a little. If I would have come in in the seventh or eighth inning, it would have been a different story, but by the time I got in, I was relaxed. I was making plans to go home (after Harrisburg's season had ended). Then they told me to break those plans because there was a possibility Buffalo would need some relief help. They were right."

Jones, who later was a teammate of Minor's with the New York Mets, said the

JOHN CANGELOSI

Throughout his baseball career Cangelosi was the guy everyone overlooked. Scouts didn't refer to him as a "can't-miss" prospect, they just said he "can't" do this and he "can't" do that.

"I've always been an underdog," Cangelosi said in 1986 when he beat long odds and laughed in the faces of all those scouts who said he couldn't make it when he earned a roster spot with the Chicago White Sox. "People always said: 'Who's that little guy? He can't play.' But I always strived hard. I'd make 'em turn around and look again."

Cangelosi was a 5-foot-8, 150-pound outfielder with the odd make-up of being a left-handed thrower and right-handed batter. "I'm a freak," he said. "I'm not small. I'm just small for the sport. My size stopped me from being drafted in high school. But college and pro ball are more competitive. There, you'll play as long as you put stats on the board. My size might hurt me if I were a home run hitter or a first baseman, but I'm qualified to do the things I do – the stolen base, play the outfield, get on base, make things happen."

Cangelosi – who began his pro career with Niagara Falls in the New York-Penn League in 1982 and stole 45 bases in 56 games – played only 139 games with the Bisons during stints in 1985, 1988 and 1990, but when he was in Buffalo, he made things happen.

When the Pirates sent him down in 1990, Cangelosi hit .348 and stole 15 bases in 24 games to help the Bisons' push for the American Association Eastern Division crown. Buffalo tied Nashville for the top spot, only to lose the division in a one-game playoff that lasted 18 innings.

That was the last game Cangelosi played for Buffalo before continuing a journey that resulted in him playing for 16 different major and minor league teams before his retirement in 1999. During his major league career Cangelosi played in 1,038 games for the White Sox, Pirates, Rangers, Astros, Marlins and Rockies, and he won a World Series ring with the 1997 Marlins. He batted .250 for his career with 154 stolen bases. In 793 minor league games, he batted .291 with 340 stolen bases. Not bad for a guy who supposedly couldn't do anything.

two occasionally talked about this game. "Freak things had been happening all night," said Jones. "Anything that could go wrong for both teams seemed to. I remember the double. It was after midnight but it seemed like it was 3 in the morning. I didn't care if the game went 30 innings, I loved it. It was the best game I've ever been associated with."

Lost in Jones' heroics was the fact that Nashville reliever Charlie Mitchell pitched the final seven innings, allowing just four hits and a walk while striking out four. He retired the last 10 Buffalo hitters and needed just five pitches to close out the game in the 18th.

The man who made the last out for the Bisons was pitcher Hugh Kemp who had come in to pitch in the 18th. Kemp had played the previous season with Nashville, and this turned out to be his final game as he retired the following spring. He flied out to center to end the game. "I knew every single person on that team," Kemp said. "Did I just want to win because of them? No. It didn't matter. We had our chances but the whole thing was kind of surreal."

Bisons owner Bob Rich Jr. – who earlier that day had submitted his expansion application to the National League office and at the time was confident Buffalo would be in the major leagues within a few years – remembers this game with fondness despite the disappointing conclusion. "That night was probably as pure a baseball moment as you'll find in Buffalo, just a really pure sporting event," Rich said. "It's not remembered in a negative way like a Wide Right or No Goal thing. It was just a tremendous game. It reminded me of (late baseball commissioner) Bart Giamatti's words, 'Baseball is a game designed to break your heart.' That's exactly what happened."

Nashville went on to lose the AA championship series to Omaha, three games to one. Incredibly, the Sounds played another marathon just three days later at home, losing 8-7 in 20 innings in a game that – including a two-hour rain delay – took six hours, 25 minutes to complete. The Bisons' 85 victories in 1990 were the most by a non-playoff team in the AA since 1944. While they won four less games in 1991, that was enough to win the Eastern Division crown and erase the frustration of the previous year. However, Buffalo lost a thrilling championship series to Denver, three games to two. Another downer in 1991: Rich lost out on his attempt at procuring a major league expansion team when Denver and Miami were selected as baseball's newest cities.

January 20, 1991 – Orchard Park, N.Y.
Rich Stadium

51-3

Al Davis still shudders whenever the subject is broached. The Darth Vader of the NFL, the patriarch of the Raiders franchise, still has nightmares relating to the events of January 1991 when the Bills dealt his proud and storied team its most devastating loss ever, a 51-3 shellacking in the AFC Championship Game. While the Houston comeback stands as the Bills' greatest achievement, this triumph over the Raiders is the team's signature victory.

More times than they'd be willing to admit, the Buffalo Bills sat in the team meeting room the night before a game looking like they were listening to coach Marv Levy, but all the while they were staring right through the old sage.

He'd spin a wonderful yarn about Winston Churchill or recite one of his many quippy quotations, and along the way he'd drop in a few words that very few of his players even knew existed. "Look it up, Thurman" he laughingly told the star running back when he used the word "enigmatic" in his presentation speech for Jim Kelly's induction to the Pro Football Hall of Fame, poking fun at the many blank stares he'd gotten from Thurman and his mates through the years.

And while in some way, on some level, the players knew that whatever Levy was talking about pertained to football, they didn't always grasp the correlation. At least not right away.

"Sometimes when he talks to us, I wish I had a dictionary in my pocket," strong safety Leonard Smith once said. "But just when you say to yourself, 'Huh?' he gives you the meaning. He doesn't leave you hanging."

Levy delivered one such Marvism in training camp prior to the start of the magical 1990 season, and it struck such a chord with linebacker Shane Conlan that right before the start of that year's AFC Championship Game against the Los Angeles Raiders, Conlan felt compelled to repeat it.

"My father was in the Marines in World War I, and he was in a famous battle, the Battle of Belleau Wood," Levy recalled. "He had a commanding officer, a major named 'Hard' John Hughes who used to say, 'When it's too tough for them, it's just right for us.' So I had told (the team) this story one hot day in training camp and I hadn't mentioned it much since. But before the kickoff, we gathered the team together on the sidelines and Shane Conlan said, 'Coach, can I say something?' And he said, 'When it's too tough for them, it's just right for us.' And I think our team took that attitude into the game."

For the next three hours on that unforgettable afternoon when Allied bombs fell on Baghdad and Jim Kelly's bombs filled the air at Rich Stadium, it was historically tough for the Raiders, and it was always just right for the Bills. Levy's cerebrally-motivated players played the game of their lives in dealing the Silver and Black a mind-boggling 51-3 defeat to clinch their first Super Bowl berth.

"We're going to The Show, baby," linebacker Darryl Talley said as he hugged team owner Ralph Wilson in the locker room. "We're going to The Show."

It couldn't have been a more glorious, yet poignant day for Wilson. Yes, his team was finally going to the Super Bowl as it pummeled his old rival from the renegade AFL days, Al Davis, with a devastating display of power and precision, the 48-point margin of victory the third-largest in playoff history. But Wilson's elation was tempered by the fact that the United States had just become embroiled in the Persian Gulf War, and it was not lost on Wilson that as the Bills and Raiders were playing a football game, fellow Americans were fighting a much more important battle in a desert halfway around the world.

A World War II veteran who served his country proudly, Wilson had tears in his eyes as he surveyed the patriotic, flag-waving, record crowd of 80,324 during the emotional playing of the National Anthem by the West Point marching band. And as the throng chanted "U-S-A!, U-S-A!, U-S-A!" he felt genuine respect in his heart for those who had been called on to carry out Operation Desert Storm.

"We are all thinking about the brave men and women over in the Gulf showing so much courage and resolve," Wilson said. "Jack Kemp (Wilson's old Buffalo quarterback

(Jamie Germano/Rochester Democrat and Chronicle)

There were many great days in the career of Pro Football Hall of Famer Jim Kelly, but one of his most memorable was the 1990 AFC Championship Game when he threw for 300 yards and two touchdowns to lead the Bills to a 51-3 demolition of the Los Angeles Raiders. The victory propelled the Bills into their first Super Bowl.

who at this time was President Bush the elder's U.S. housing secretary) called me a few days ago and said the troops over there wanted the games to be played. That's why the league has gone on with them, because that's what the troops want."

There had been doubt, though, right up until the final hours before kickoff whether the AFC and NFC Championship games would go on. Four days earlier Bush said "The battle has been joined," as he gave the OK to begin the bombing raids on strategic targets in Iraq and occupied Kuwait.

(Shawn Dowd/Rochester Democrat and Chronicle)

During his fabulous 15-year career with the Bills Bruce Smith recorded a team-record 171 sacks, and by the time the 2003 NFL season is over, Smith, now a member of the Washington Redskins, will likely be the NFL's all-time leading sacker.

Fearing retaliatory terrorist strikes in the U.S. by Saddam Hussein, the NFL thought long and hard about postponing the game in Buffalo and the NFC title match later that afternoon in San Francisco between the 49ers and Giants. After all, what better place to make a political statement than at a nationally-televised sporting event where more than 80,000 people had gathered?

"We recognize that the American people will not be paralyzed by the events in the Middle East or allow the fabric of our daily life to be destroyed," NFL commissioner Paul Tagliabue said. "We will obviously follow the events in the Middle East and take those into account as we approach kickoff. If the networks believe that the events in the Gulf are so dramatic or so significant that they should go to an all-news format, then we would not play our games."

The domestic threats proved to be unfounded and with security tighter than it ever had been for a game in Orchard Park, the game went on, which was really too bad for the Raiders.

The Bills won the opening coin toss – no surprise on this day – and they proceeded to run their no-huddle offense to perfection. They had the Raiders gasping so badly for air that after Buffalo had advanced 55 yards in five lightning-quick plays, the Raiders called for a timeout to regroup and catch their collective breath.

"That was the greatest feeling that I've ever had in a game other than putting points on the board," center Kent Hull said. "They told us right there that the only way we can stop you is with a timeout. We were laughing in the huddle."

Said Kelly: "I remember (Raiders defensive lineman) Howie Long telling me on that drive, 'Come on, Jim, slow down.' We were probably the most well-conditioned team offensively in the league. It was more than a two-minute drill. It was a sprint. We knew some games we'd play against big guys very good at stopping the run, and we wanted to get 'em tired."

Four plays later, Kelly dropped a shotgun snap, but was still able to throw a 13-yard touchdown pass to James Lofton and you knew something was up. The rout was on.

Los Angeles showed its only spark when it touched the ball for the first time. Quarterback Jay Schroeder completed a pair of 26-yard passes to Mervyn Fernandez and Willie Gault, but the Buffalo defense rose up and forced the Raiders to settle for a 41-yard Jeff Jaeger field goal. Any hope the Raiders had of staying competitive was blown away in the next few minutes. It took Kelly just four plays after the kickoff to put another touchdown on the board as he hit Lofton for a 41-yard gain before Thomas skipped into the end zone on a 12-yard run.

After a Raiders punt the Bills were on the move again, driving to the Los Angeles 24 before Kelly threw an interception to Garry Lewis. Not to worry. Disappointed groans turned to wild cheers a minute later when Talley picked off a Schroeder pass and raced 27 yards for a touchdown. There was still more than 48 minutes to play and the Bills were ahead 21-3.

Levy remembered the impact that play had on the rest of the game. His Bills were thrilled, but they remained resolute, while Art Shell's Raiders seemed to shrivel. "When something like that happens, the other team begins to press," Levy said. "Our guys stayed very focused, they didn't get giddy on the sidelines."

Things only got worse for the Raiders. Another punt led to another touchdown drive by the Bills. Los Angeles, shell-shocked by Kelly's no-huddle passing, went almost exclusively to a dime defense, so Kelly decided to stick to the ground and he handed off to Thomas and Kenneth Davis on delays and counters out of the shotgun. "We were always one step ahead of them," Kelly said. This time it was 57 yards in 13 plays with Davis crashing in from the 1 on fourth down. Although Scott Norwood's extra point was blocked, it was 27-3.

The count could have risen again when Los Angeles' Ron Holland muffed the kickoff and Jamie Mueller recovered at the Raiders' 27, but Norwood missed a 45-yard field goal.

Pfffttt.

Like it mattered. The Bills' defense forced another punt, and Kelly's 44-yard strike to Steve Tasker led to Davis' three-yard TD run to make it 34-3.

Still not ready to call off the attack, Nate Odomes intercepted a Schroeder pass and returned it to the Raiders 39, setting up Kelly's eight-yard TD pass to Lofton 1:06 before the end of the half.

As the Bills left the field at intermission to a resounding ovation, their 41 first-half points a new NFL playoff record, the grounds crew down at Tampa Stadium – site

DARRYL TALLEY

The headlines were reserved for Jim Kelly, Thurman Thomas, Bruce Smith and Andre Reed. But if you ask any of those former Bills' greats who the heart and soul of the Buffalo dynasty in the early 1990s was, to a man they will name Talley.

He came to the Bills as a second-round draft choice out of West Virginia in 1983, and after a few difficult years trying to find his niche with the team, Talley became a full-time starter in 1986. From that point on, he began forging a career that arguably ranks him as the best linebacker in the history of the team.

"Darryl is the most consistent linebacker in the league and I'll never stop saying it," Talley's good buddy, Smith, once said. That's because while Talley wasn't a flashy player who made huge, game-changing plays, he did all the little things that often guaranteed victory.

"When I come to play, I'm bringing my lunch bucket because I'm going to be here all day whether you like it or not," Talley once said of his relentless style. "I'm not going to leave and I'm not going to run. I'm going to stand there and go toe-to-toe with whoever they bring out."

During three of the four Super Bowl years Talley was Buffalo's leading tackler, and during his 12-year tenure, the Bills played 204 games counting the postseason, and he played in every single one, a team record for consecutive games played that may never be broken.

When he was released in a salary cap move following the 1994 season, Talley showed a touch of class by taking out an advertisement in the *Buffalo News* to thank the fans of Western New York. His statement read in part: "In leaving Buffalo, I want to express my sincerest thanks to everyone who has made my 12 years here the most memorable time of my life. I will go away with only fond memories. To the people of Buffalo, thanks for making me feel like one of your own. On behalf of my family, thanks for the memories. It was my honor."

of the following week's Super Bowl – got busy. There was no need to wait for this game to end. It was over, so they began painting "BILLS" in one of the end zones.

The second half was a mere formality. Davis added his third touchdown run of the day, Norwood kicked a 39-yard field goal, and the defense protected the sanctity of the slaughter by blanking the Raiders with the help of three more interceptions of Schroeder.

When the carnage was complete, 18 championship game records had been set including most first downs (30) and highest completion percentage by a quarterback as Kelly, in throwing for 300 yards, completed 17 of 23 for 73.9 percent. Thomas finished with 138 yards rushing and another 61 receiving, and Lofton had five catches for 113 yards as the Bills amassed 502 total yards.

"Not in my wildest dreams did I think we'd score 51 points against these guys," said Kelly.

Defensively, the Bills recorded six interceptions and seven turnovers, and held Marcus Allen to 26 yards rushing. "We had the kind of day where it seemed we couldn't do anything right," said Schroeder.

In the locker room, as the Bills celebrated their first AFC/AFL title since 1965, Talley recalled the horror of Buffalo's back-to-back 2-14 seasons in the mid-1980s. "I went through the jokes, you know, like 'Knock, knock. Who's there? Owen. Owen who? Oh-and-10.' Yeah, I thought about the bad years. You'd go out in public and people would be snickering and laughing at you behind your back. I just tried to play as hard as I could during those times and I hoped that eventually better times would come."

Happy days were here for Talley and the Bills. And there was hope for the happiest day of all when, one week hence, they would play in Super Bowl 25.

"I've been to almost every Super Bowl and every time I'm there, I daydream," Wilson said. "When the players would run out on the field, electricity would fill the stadium and I'd think 'Boy, wouldn't it be great if someday the Bills were able to run out of that tunnel on a Super Bowl Sunday.' I'm a little shell-shocked by the tremendous performance the team put on today. This is probably the best performance the Bills have ever had. Anything in the last 31 years that didn't go the right way, it was all turned around today." And then it turned back around in Tampa. Instead of it being the happiest day in team history it became the saddest when Norwood missed a 47-yard field goal with four seconds remaining and the Bills lost the championship game to the Giants, 20-19. The Bills would go on to win four consecutive AFC championships, a record that may never be broken, and they would go on to lose every Super Bowl, another record that may never be broken. It was a time of ultimate highs and ultimate lows for this franchise, and 51-3 was the highest of the highs. One more time: 51-3.

January 27, 1991 – Tampa, Fla.
Tampa Stadium

Wide Right

Just one week after registering their signature victory, the Bills endured their signature defeat. Of all the losses this team has had to cope with in 43 years of operation, it is safe to assume that none carried the everlasting heartbreak of the Super Bowl 25 setback when Scott Norwood's potential winning field goal sailed wide right, denying the Bills a victory over Bill Parcells' New York Giants at Tampa Stadium.

When it's Super Bowl week, the phones at NFL Films ring incessantly. It has become a yearly rite of passage at the company's New Jersey offices, this deluge of requests from television networks and their affiliates for footage of Super Bowls past to fill their vast array of pre-game shows and specials.

Certain clips get more play than others: Joe Namath running off the Orange Bowl field with his forefinger held high after beating the Baltimore Colts in Super Bowl 3; Lynn Swann's acrobatic catch for Pittsburgh in Super Bowl 10; Marcus Allen's brilliant change-of-direction 74-yard touchdown run for the Raiders in Super Bowl 18; and of course the instant classic, Adam Vinatieri's game-winning 48-yard field goal for the Patriots in Super Bowl 36.

Oh yeah, there's another clip, another moment forever frozen on celluloid and digitally re-mastered, that NFL Films President Steve Sabol never stops getting requests for, and any Bills' fan worth his Zubaz pants, red, white and blue face paint and insulated boots knows what it is: The Miss. Wide Right. Norwide.

"Requests shoot up during Super Bowl time," Sabol said a few years ago of Scott Norwood's 47-yard field goal attempt that sailed wide right at Tampa Stadium, preventing the Bills from defeating the New York Giants in Super Bowl 25. "It tends to get replayed a lot at this time of year."

Bills fans wish Sabol would destroy the footage of the single-greatest disappointment in their team's history, in Buffalo sports history. Instead, there it is, every year in late January, taunting and tormenting the Super Bowl-starved denizens of Western New York. They will watch it over and over and over, and close their eyes and dream about what it might have felt like had the kick nuzzled its way between the uprights and given the Bills the ultimate victory.

Buffalo. Super Bowl champions. Oh, the glory.

Oh, the reality.

Sabol could make like Hitchcock or Spielberg and pull off some special effect thereby making that ball soar through cleanly, but the result will never change. Giants 20, Bills 19. Ultimate victory is still ultimate defeat.

"They hammer away showing that thing," Bills owner Ralph Wilson said of the constant replaying of Wide Right. "I grimace every time I see it. I'm sure Scott does, too."

He does. Norwood has moved on, and Wide Right has not ruined his life. He turned 43 years old in 2003, he is married to a former West Seneca girl, lives in Northern Virginia with her and their three children, and works as a financial adviser. His life is good. But it's not humanly possible to forget the worst professional moment of your life, and Norwood hasn't.

"It wasn't a short one by any means," Norwood said of the field goal that is still the only win-or-else attempt in Super Bowl history (remember, Vinatieri's winner came with a tie score, as did Jim O'Brien's for Baltimore in Super Bowl 5). "My stance has always been that I was there to kick the ball. In that instance, I didn't do my job and I didn't get my job done. I take responsibility for that."

Although it has been easy these last 12 years to blame Norwood for the loss, it has never been fair. Yes, his job was to kick the ball, and on that particular kick, he failed. However, Norwood's teammates certainly did their share to sabotage Buffalo's best chance at Super Bowl glory.

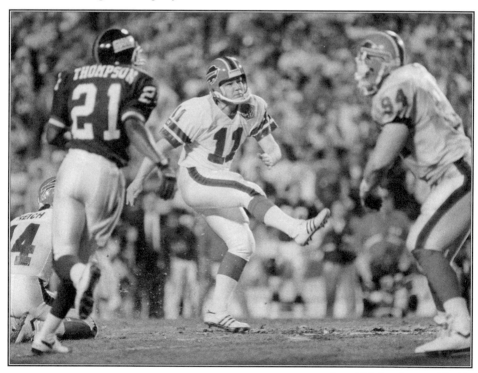

(Annette Lein/Rochester Democrat and Chronicle)

Super Bowl XXV came down to this moment - Scott Norwood's 47-yard yard field goal attempt with four seconds left to play. The kick sailed right allowing the New York Giants to become NFL champions.

"The disappointing thing was that we should not have been in that position to begin with, it didn't come down to the kick," said center Kent Hull. "We had our troubles before all that. We did everything opposite of what got us here – great execution and sound defense. We didn't do any of that."

To which quarterback Jim Kelly and linebacker Darryl Talley agreed.

"They held us to 19 points and not many teams can do that," Kelly said, sounding almost amazed that the Giants had befuddled the no-huddle offense which had scored 95 points in playoff victories the previous two weeks over the Dolphins and Raiders. "Give the Giants credit, but we stopped ourselves, too. We had opportunities to put points on the board and we didn't do it. Penalties hurt, we had some dropped passes, and I made some bad reads."

Talley spoke for the defensive shortcomings in a game where the Giants ball-controlled the Bills to death for a Super Bowl-record 40 minutes, 33 seconds. "We just didn't tackle," Talley said. "We didn't play smart, we tried to do too much. It was not good football."

But it was high entertainment. The stadium was electric all day, and not just because it was Super Sunday. America had entered the Persian Gulf War two weeks earlier, and tensions were high as game-time approached. There was great fear that madman Saddam Hussein would answer the bombings in Baghdad with a terrorist strike at the Super Bowl, so Tampa went into a virtual police state with unprecedented security.

Tomahawk helicopters patrolled the skies and every person entering the stadium walked through metal detectors and was subject to a body search. Emotions were stirred during pre-game warm-ups when scenes of U.S. soldiers doing their country proud were flashed on the Jumbotron, and then patriotic fervor reached a crescendo when Whitney Houston belted out a stirring rendition of the *Star-Spangled Banner* punctuated by fighter jets roaring overhead in a fly-over as more than 73,000 fans waved tiny American flags.

It was a scene that no one who was there will ever forget. Goose bumps abounded, and there was a sense that these two teams might struggle in this bubbling cauldron. But then the game began and those notions were quickly muted. The Bills and Giants attacked each other with a fury and the fans loved it. So many Super Bowls had died under the weight of hype. This one thrived, and for three glorious hours, America's attention was diverted.

"It was an incredible experience, the emotion of the whole thing," tight end Pete Metzelaars recalled. "It was during Desert Storm and all that stuff was going on. So that was all stacked up on it also."

After the Giants took an early 3-0 lead on Matt Bahr's 28-yard field goal, Kelly connected with James Lofton on a 61-yard pass to position the Bills on the New York 8, but two Kelly incompletions forced Buffalo to settle for Norwood's tying 23-yard field goal.

THURMAN THOMAS

The award went to Ottis Anderson of the New York Giants, but Thomas was the most valuable player in Super Bowl 25. Anderson had an excellent game, but Thomas was better. It's a fact.

If Scott Norwood had made the 47-yard field goal at the end of the game to deliver the victory to Buffalo, Thomas would have been a unanimous choice for MVP. He was the best player on the field that day, and very often during his fabulous career he was the best player whenever he was on the field.

Someday Thomas' name will come up during a Pro Football Hall of Fame voting meeting, and someone will probably point out that Thomas never won an NFL rushing crown, and he never won a Super Bowl. At that point, the rest of the voters should laugh heartily, then write Thomas' name on their ballot, because his resume is virtually without peer.

For four years (1989-92), he led the NFL in total yards gained from scrimmage, a feat unprecedented in NFL history. He soared past Hall of Famer O.J. Simpson's team rushing record in 1996, he had eight consecutive 1,000-yard seasons, and when he retired from the NFL after the 2001 season, he was ninth on the all-time league rushing list with 12,074 yards and sixth in yards gained from scrimmage (16,532). In the postseason, no one has scored more touchdowns (21) than Thomas and his 1,432 playoff rushing yards is third-best.

During one of the interview sessions prior to Super Bowl 26, Thomas made a case that he was the Michael Jordan of the Bills' offense, and Jim Kelly agreed. "Thurman was the key to my success," the Hall of Fame quarterback said. "I knew where my bread was buttered. In order to run the no-huddle offense you had to have a back who could do everything, and that was Thurman."

After spending one season with Miami, Thomas signed a one-day contract in 2001 so that he could retire properly as a Bill. That day, he said "I just wanted to win. When I was in that locker room I wanted my teammates to feel like they could count on me at all times."

They always did.

The Bills then seemed to take command of the game in the second quarter as Kelly – at his no-huddling best – engineered a 12-play, 80-yard drive that included four passes to Andre Reed for 44 yards. Little-used running back Don Smith culminated the march with a one-yard touchdown plunge.

Two possessions later Rick Tuten pinned the Giants back to their 7 with a 43-yard punt, and after a holding penalty on center Bart Oates pushed New York closer to its own goal line, quarterback Jeff Hostetler made a big mistake. In dropping back into the end zone to attempt a pass, Hostetler stumbled to the ground and Bruce Smith fell on him for a safety to give the Bills a 12-3 lead.

With momentum clearly on their side, the Bills could have buried the Giants after the free kick, but their next two possessions resulted in Tuten punts, and after the second, Hostetler trotted onto the field with 3:49 left in the half. The Giants needed a spark, and the man who was filling in for injured starter Phil Simms provided it.

Hostetler, who had been unable to get much working to this point, suddenly found his groove. He completed 5 of 8 passes during an 87-yard march, the last a 14-yard scoring toss to Stephen Baker with 25 seconds left in the half. And then New York received the second-half kickoff and embarked on a remarkable touchdown drive that consumed the first 9:29 of the third quarter. The 14-play, 75-yard journey was marked by a number of big plays, none bigger than Hostetler's 14-yard completion to Mark

Ingram on a third-and-13 from the Buffalo 32 on which the Bills missed about five tackles. Eventually, O.J. Anderson crashed across the goal line from the 1 to give the Giants a 17-12 lead.

"Our whole plan was to shorten the game for Buffalo," said Giants coach Bill Parcells. "We wanted the ball and we didn't want them to have it."

That's because Parcells knew how dangerous Buffalo's quick-strike offense was, and his worst fears were soon realized. Late in the third quarter Smith stuffed Anderson on a fourth-down play at the Bills 37, and Kelly – who had been on the field less than two minutes in the third quarter – rode the momentum swing to the go-ahead touchdown early in the fourth. He completed three quick passes for 32 yards, then watched as Thurman Thomas swept around right end for a 31-yard touchdown that put the Bills on top 19-17.

All that hard work by the Giants, and they were still trailing. So Hostetler came back out after David Meggett returned the kickoff to the 23, and he started another interminable march. This one chewed up 7:32 as the Giants seemed to cover ground one blade of grass at a time before Bahr kicked what turned out to be a winning 21-yard field goal with 7:20 left.

(Annette Lein/Rochester Democrat and Chronicle)

Although he didn't win the award, there was no doubt Thurman Thomas was the MVP of Super Bowl XXV as he produced 190 yards of total offense. By the time Thomas' Buffalo career ended in 1999, he was the Bills' all-time leading rusher with 11,398 yards.

The teams exchanged punts, and that left Buffalo at its own 10-yard-line with 2:16 to go. Kelly entered the huddle and said "This is what champions are made of, let's be one."

On first down, he was forced to scramble for eight yards and that brought us to the two-minute warning. After the timeout, Kelly scrambled again, this time gaining just one yard, bringing up third-and-one. From the shotgun he handed off to Thomas who sped left and rambled 22 yards to the 41 as a huge roar from the Buffalo contingent pierced the warm Tampa air.

A four-yard pass to Reed and another scramble by Kelly produced a first down at the Giants 46 and Kelly called his final timeout with 48 seconds remaining. Norwood had already begun preparing himself for a potential attempt, and he admitted it was "a great feeling" to know the game might come down to a swing of his right leg. He wasn't rooting for a touchdown. He wanted the opportunity to win the game.

"If you're hoping for them to score a touchdown that means you're not focused," he said. "My job is to go out there and kick the field goal, it's the only thought on my mind. If something else happens, that's fine, but I'm focused on the kick."

Even though he could not stop the clock, Kelly threw a ball to Keith McKeller in the middle of the field, and the tight end made a shoestring catch before being tackled after a six-yard gain. The Bills caught a break when time was called to review the play to make sure McKeller made the catch, and when the catch was upheld, Kelly quickly set his teammates, then handed off to Thomas. Thomas' last carry of a superb 190-yard total offense day netted 11 yards to the 29, but when Mark Collins tackled him in bounds, the Bills were not going to be able to run another play. Kelly hustled to the line and spiked the ball to stop the clock with eight ticks left.

"I had positive thoughts," Norwood said. "I don't back away from kicks like this. It's something I've done my whole career. It's a kick I've made."

Just not on this night.

"I kept my head down good on it, but I saw the ball wasn't drawing in like normal," Norwood said. "I've kicked enough footballs to know. It was an empty feeling watching it hang out there."

The next day more than 30,000 Buffalonians came to Niagara Square to welcome the team back from Tampa. It was another scene that will never be forgotten as the player who received the greatest applause was Norwood. As he spoke to the gathering, tears rolled down his cheeks, and years later, he explained why. "I wasn't so much hurting because of the kick itself," Norwood said. "The kick was about the people. It wasn't about anything else. It wasn't about monetary gain or some great stature for myself or anything else. When you talk about the Buffalo Bills, it really is about the community and the people who support it. They had a lot of emotions invested in us. It was an emotional time. I just felt bad for the people."

September 8, 1991 – Denver, Colo.
Mile High Stadium

Eight Wasn't Enough

Perhaps the 1992 Bills drew the inspiration needed for their miracle comeback against the Houston Oilers by watching the Bisons almost pull off a miracle comeback in the American Association championship series 16 months earlier. Down 9-0 and being no-hit through eight innings, the Bisons erupted for eight runs in the top of the ninth at Denver's Mile High Stadium, only to see the rally die a painful and controversial death when Greg Edge was thrown out at the plate to the end the game while trying to score the tying run.

On the occasion of his induction into the Buffalo Baseball Hall of Fame in 1999, former Bisons' play-by-play announcer Pete Weber reminisced about one of the most bizarre games he ever called.

In so doing, he offered an editorial comment regarding the Bisons' 9-8 loss to the Denver Zephyrs in Game 4 of the 1991 American Association championship series at Mile High Stadium when Buffalo's Greg Edge was dramatically thrown out at home – allegedly – to end the game.

"To my dying day in front of you, I will swear on every holy book known to man that Edge had his foot on home plate before he was tagged," Weber said, his words greeted with a rousing round of applause.

Too bad umpire Scott Potter disagreed with Weber. When Potter emphatically punched the air and ruled that Denver catcher Joe Kmak tagged Edge who was trying to score the tying run from first base on a double by Greg Tubbs, he short-circuited one of the greatest ninth-inning rallies ever.

And we're not just talking Bisons history. We're not talking minor league history. We're talking baseball history.

"It was crazy," said D.L. Smith, a journeyman infielder who that night watched the proceedings from the bullpen as the designated bullpen catcher for the Zephyrs. "Nobody could believe it. What a game!"

For eight innings Smith sat on the bench out in the pen and played the role of spectator, just like the 4,103 fans who were in attendance. He had nothing better to do because Denver's starting pitcher, Greg Mathews, held the Bisons without a hit while his teammates were running up a seemingly insurmountable 9-0 lead.

When Mathews took the mound in the ninth, the only issue in doubt was whether the left-hander was going to register the first nine-inning no-hitter in Mile High Stadium history. Pretty soon Smith became the busiest guy in the ballpark, while Mathews and the rest of the Zephyrs began to wonder if Buffalo was going to walk off the field as American Association champions.

"I think I warmed up just about everybody on the team – all in the ninth inning," Smith quipped.

The Bisons, offensively inept all night, suddenly sprang to life and put together a stunning rally against Mathews and four other Denver pitchers to score eight runs on nine hits, and by the time they were halted by Potter's questionable call, not a heart was beating, not a breath was being drawn.

"I've been involved in some wild games before, but this is the craziest I've ever seen," said Denver manager Tony Muser, who gleefully high-tailed it off the field, opting not to stick around to watch the Bisons go ballistic on Potter.

One of the most vociferous protesters was Buffalo catcher Jeff Banister who bumped Potter during the post-game melee and also threw a chair. He was suspended by Triple-A Alliance commissioner Randy Mobley, fined $250 for his actions, and had to

(Buffalo Bisons)

Greg Edge's Bisons' career was a short one, but he was in Buffalo long enough to play a key role in one of the team's most memorable games. It was Edge who was thrown out at the plate for the final out of the game, cutting short a dramatic ninth-inning Buffalo rally in the 1991 American Association championship series at Denver.

sit out the deciding game of the series the next night.

"That was probably the greatest comeback I've ever been involved with or ever seen," Banister said. "Going into the top of the ninth down 9-0 and the guy's throwing a no-hitter. I hate to lose, and to lose one like that, to have a ballgame decided on a play at the plate ... In my heart, I honestly believe Greg got to the plate and was safe. I don't know if I bumped anyone or not, it was a blur. Everything happened so fast, I guess my emotions got to me."

He wasn't alone. The entire team rushed onto the field to vehemently argue the call. Manager Terry Collins erupted into a profanity-laced tirade with umpire crew chief Perry Costello. And Bisons' general manager Mike Billoni confronted the umpires outside their dressing room and like Banister, he was fined and prohibited from going on the field before or during Game 5.

Not that any of their venting mattered. Potter's call stood, the series was tied at two games apiece, and somehow the Bisons were faced with the unenviable task of trying to put the loss behind them and win the fifth game the next night, which, by the way, they were unable to do.

The Bisons, division winners for the first time since 1959, hosted the first two games of the best-of-five championship series at Pilot Field and won both by identical 4-1 scores with Game 2 played in front of a sellout crowd of 21,050. After that game, Billoni thanked the huge throng for their support, then all but guaranteed that the Bisons would go out to Denver, finish the job, and bring back to Buffalo the first minor league baseball championship since 1961 when the Bisons won the International League title and the Little World Series.

Needing just one victory to wrap it up, the Bisons flew confidently to Denver to resume the series the next night, but they stumbled in Game 3 and lost 8-3 as they hit into an American Association record-tying six double plays.

With his team back in the series, Muser had a decision to make on his starting pitcher. He could go with his ace, 13-game winner and AA strikeout leader Cal Eldred, on three days rest, or go with Mathews whose turn it was to pitch. He chose Mathews. "We've kept Cal in the same rotation all year and I'm not going to mess with it now," Muser said.

After leading Cal-State Fullerton to the 1984 College World Series championship, Mathews broke into the majors with the Cardinals in 1986 and won 11 games, the most by a St. Louis rookie in 15 years. In 1987 he went 11-11, won Game 1 of the National League Championship Series against San Francisco, and started Game 4 of the World Series against Minnesota, leaving with a no-decision in a game St. Louis ultimately won.

He was a star in the making. But a quadriceps injury cost him half a season on the disabled list in 1988, and major elbow surgery in 1989 nearly ended his career. A comeback in 1990 was a disaster so the Cardinals released him, and after signing with Kansas City, he was quickly cut in the spring of 1991. Nearing the end of the line,

Mathews signed with Milwaukee and agreed to start in Single-A Beloit, Wis. By mid-season he was in Denver and a key member of Muser's rotation.

However, in his last start, with a chance to clinch the Western Division title, Mathews was routed by Oklahoma City and hadn't pitched since. It didn't take long to realize that Mathews had shaken off that outing and was back in form. The Bisons

---

TERRY COLLINS

Collins proved his worth as a manager during his stellar three-year stint with the Bisons between 1989 and 1991, but ask him what the key was to landing his first major league managerial job with Houston in 1994 and he points to the time he spent coaching under Jim Leyland.

"When you work for a Jim Leyland there is a credibility that comes with it," said Collins, who was Leyland's bullpen coach with the Pittsburgh Pirates in 1992 and '93. "When I went to Houston, they said, `Here's a guy who has some experience as a minor league manager, and he's been a major league coach under Jim Leyland.'

"When I went up to Pittsburgh, Jim showed me what it takes to manage in the bigs and then he let me watch and listen while he did his job. That was a great learning experience for me. It's all about how you treat people. I learned a lot of that from Jim."

Collins was a light-hitting but gritty minor-league shortstop who played 11 years in the Pirates and Dodgers organizations before turning to managing. He managed Albuquerque, the Dodgers' Triple-A team in the Pacific Coast League, for five years before coming to Buffalo, winning *The Sporting News* Minor League Manager of the Year Award in 1987 when the Dukes won the PCL title.

Collins took over a Bisons team that hadn't finished better than third since moving up to the triple-A American Association in 1985 and compiled a winning percentage of .549. His first two teams finished second in the Eastern Division, the 1990 club losing an 18-inning division playoff game, and in 1991, Buffalo won the East before losing the AA championship series to Denver. His success earned him induction into the Buffalo Baseball Hall of Fame, as well as a promotion by the Pirates.

At the major league level, his intensity rubbed some of the Astros the wrong way and despite three straight second-place finishes in the NL Central he was fired. He moved on to Anaheim in 1997 and his Angels finished above .500 and in second place in the AL West his first two years, but the team struggled badly his third season and he resigned in September, paving the way for Mike Scioscia to take over the club.

---

couldn't touch him and at one point Mathews retired 19 men in succession.

Buffalo's starter, Kevin Blankenship, couldn't match Mathews, though he didn't pitch terribly. He gave up five runs in 5 1/3 innings, but he left trailing just 2-0. Denver loaded the bases in the sixth so Collins relieved Blankenship with Tim Meeks and Meeks was promptly tagged for a grand slam by Kmak that gave Denver a 6-0 lead, three of the runs charged to Blankenship.

The lead had ballooned to 9-0 when Buffalo came to bat in the ninth, and with the crowd – if you can call it that compared to the massive gatherings at Pilot Field – in a frenzy, Mathews prepared to work against Banister. First pitch fastball, no-hitter done as Banister rifled a double to right-center and now it was just another 9-0 game. Or so everyone thought.

Jeff Richardson, Tubbs and Armando Moreno followed with singles which plated two runs and chased Mathews to the dugout. After a fielders' choice grounder by Keith Miller, Brian Dorsett ripped a three-run homer to cut Buffalo's deficit to 9-5.

"It was a great game up to that point," Smith said. "Then it was a crazy game."

Said Kmak: "I just kept looking at the scoreboard. It was 9-2, then it was 9-5. It was getting scary."

It was only the beginning.

Joe Redfield beat out a chopper in front of the plate, Eddie Zambrano reached base when Denver third baseman Charlie Montoyo threw wide of second trying to get a force, and pinch-hitter Ty Gainey flared a single to right to load the bases. Brian Fischer, the third Denver pitcher of the inning, struck out Tim Hines for the second out, but Edge kept the rally alive by beating out an infield single off reliever Tim Fortugno which allowed Redfield to score. On that play, Denver shortstop Pat Listach's throw appeared to nail Edge by an edge, but first base umpire Kevin O'Connor ruled in favor of Buffalo and it was 9-6, bases still loaded, still two outs. That brought Tubbs back for his second at-bat of the inning, this time against Denver's fifth pitcher of the inning, right-hander Andy McGaffigan.

The count went to 2-and-1 – the strike coming on a foul ball down the right-field line that would have ended the game had Denver right-fielder Matias Carrillo made the makeable catch – and McGaffigan threw a belt-high fastball. Tubbs jumped on it, hitting a searing line drive into the left field corner.

Two runs scored, and as Mickey Brantley corralled the ball and fired in to the cutoff man at third, Montoyo, Edge was rounding third and heading home. Montoyo's relay was perfect, Kmak caught it and slapped the tag, and Potter made the blood-curdling call.

"I got to the plate, I was there," Edge said defiantly. "Right when I looked up I saw my foot dead on home plate."

Naturally, Kmak had a different viewpoint. "I think he was out, I don't think he got to home plate. I just told myself to put my body in front of the plate and hold on to the ball. There were two bang-bang plays in the inning (this and the Listach play). One of them went their way and one of them went our way."

Tubbs was left to lament how close he had come to hitting a grand slam. "I'm upset that I didn't get it out," he said. "If I could have just gotten it up, it would have gone. It was the same pitch that I hit for my other two homers (earlier in the series)."

   In the Bisons' clubhouse, Collins tried to put a positive spin on the dramatic con-clusion. "The way the game ended might have made it a high note for them," he said, perhaps only half-believing himself.

Collins was wrong. So was Redfield, the Bison third baseman who claimed that despite the loss the momentum had swung back to Buffalo thanks to the big rally. The next night Rick Reed, the Bisons' ace and the pitcher of the year in the AA, left Game 5 after just 10 pitches when he hurt his back, the Zephyrs jumped out to a 3-0 lead, and after a 64-minute rain delay, they continued on their rampage and rang up a 12-3 championship-clinching victory. Denver went on to defeat Columbus of the International league, four games to one, to win the Triple-A Alliance championship. After the 18-inning loss to Nashville in the one-game Eastern Division playoff in 1990, and this heartbreaking result, the Bisons won the East again in 1992 under new manager Marc Bombard, compiling a record of 87-57, their best since 1936, only to lose the championship series in four games to Oklahoma City. It wasn't until 1997 that the Bisons finally broke through, winning the AA championship in a three-game sweep over Iowa.

January 3, 1993 – Orchard Park, N.Y.
Rich Stadium

The Comeback

Darryl Talley asked us to "Believe, believe, believe." Yeah, right. The Bills were down 32 points to the Houston Oilers early in the third quarter of their 1992 AFC wild-card playoff game at Rich Stadium. They started the game without future Hall of Fame quarterback Jim Kelly and star linebacker Cornelius Bennett, then lost star running back Thurman Thomas for the second half due to an injury. How could Talley have chided us for not believing that the Bills could pull off the greatest comeback in NFL history? Shame on us. Shame on all of us for not believing.

Can it really be 10 years since the greatest game in Buffalo Bills history was played?

How is it possible that a decade has passed since that unbelievable afternoon at Rich Stadium when the Bills pulled off the greatest comeback the NFL has ever seen?

Check your calendars, folks. It only seems like yesterday when the Bills fell behind the Houston Oilers 35-3 two minutes into the third quarter of their AFC Wild-Card playoff game at Rich Stadium before rallying in historic and improbable and incomprehensible fashion to pull off a 41-38 overtime victory.

Seriously, 10 years have come and gone since that most glorious of occasions, and the only people working on One Bills Drive today who played in that game are defensive coordinator Jerry Gray and defensive backs coach Steve Jackson. And they played for the Oilers.

For that matter, the Oilers don't even exist. They moved to Tennessee to become the Titans, and were finally replaced in 2002 after a five-year pro football drought in Houston by the expansion Texans.

Bills coach Gregg Williams was a Houston assistant coach on the day the Oilers melted down in seismic proportions. Of course, Williams moved with the rest of the Oilers to Tennessee in 1997 and was an assistant on the day the Titans paid the Bills back for The Comeback. That was in January 2000 when Tennessee executed the infamous Home Run Throwback to beat Buffalo in another remarkable AFC Wild-Card playoff game.

When he was introduced as the Bills new head coach in February 2001, Williams said "We won't talk about Home Run Throwback if you don't talk about The Comeback."

Sorry, Gregg, but it's hard not to talk about it.

The Bills had won back-to-back AFC championships but had lost both Super Bowls, to the Giants and Redskins. They were eager to make amends, but to do so, they would have to win a third straight AFC title, something only the Miami Dolphins of the early 1970s had accomplished.

And the Bills made the road to the Super Bowl tough on themselves by losing three of the final five games in 1992, costing them a fifth straight AFC East division title and relegating them to wild-card status as Miami finished first. This meant the Bills were not exempt from the first round of the playoffs, and the run-and-shoot Oilers of Warren Moon were the designated opponent.

Making matters more difficult, the Bills would have to play Houston without star quarterback Jim Kelly and star linebacker Cornelius Bennett who were sidelined with injuries.

The Bills knew they'd be in for a battle, but no one could have foreseen just how badly things would be for Buffalo. Moon got off to a blazing start completing 19 of his 22 first-half passes for 218 yards and four touchdowns as the Oilers gushed to a seemingly insurmountable 28-3 lead.

(Wil Yurman/Rochester Democrat and Chronicle)

In what most fans rank as the greatest Bills' game ever, Steve Christie's 38-yard field goal in overtime gave Buffalo a 41-38 wild-card playoff victory over the Houston Oilers, a game the Bills were trailing 35-3 early in the third quarter. The comeback was the most prolific in NFL history.

And when cornerback Bubba McDowell picked off a Frank Reich pass and raced 58 yards to the end zone two minutes into the third quarter to make it 35-3, Buffalo's plight was downright hopeless.

"Believe, believe, believe," linebacker Darryl Talley said after Steve Christie's 32-yard field goal won the game in overtime.

Easy to say in the aftermath of a miracle, but a number of Bills admitted that winning the game was the furthest thing on their minds after McDowell pranced down the sideline while a non-sellout crowd of 74,141 looked on in stunned silence.

(Wil Yurman/Rochester Democrat and Chronicle)

Andre Reed left Buffalo in 1999 as the Bills' all-time leader in receptions (941), receiving yards (13,095) and receiving touchdowns (86). Perhaps his greatest performance came in the comeback victory over the Oilers when he caught eight passes for 136 yards and three touchdowns to key the rally.

"Of course it seemed like it was hopeless," said wide receiver Andre Reed. "Our defense was not stopping them, it seemed like they were going to run up and down the field all day on us."

There was one player, though, who knew there was still hope. That was Reich, who during his college career at Maryland engineered what was then – in 1984 – the greatest comeback in NCAA history, rallying the Terps from a 31-0 halftime deficit to a 42-40 victory over defending national champion Miami.

"Gale (Gilbert) and I told him before the second half, 'Well Frank, you had the greatest comeback in college history, let's see if you can do it in the pros' and he went out and did it," said Kelly, who had been knocked out of commission by these same Oilers a week earlier in the regular-season finale during a 27-3 loss at the Astrodome.

"In order to have a comeback like that, you have to make some big plays and I'll tell you, the poise that Frank showed out there, I don't think it can be matched. That was the greatest win I've ever been associated with and I was on the sidelines. It doesn't feel good standing there, but when a guy like Frank pulls through, that's great."

Said Reich: "Your thought is to take it one play at a time and don't try to force anything. In thinking back to the experience in college, it wasn't any great thing that I did. We only threw 15 times in the second half in that game and we were down 31 points so I knew it could be done. I wasn't thinking in terms of winning, I was thinking of taking it one play at a time."

ANDRE REED

The first time Elbert Dubenion saw Reed, he wanted to enroll him in the FBI's witness protection program so no other National Football League scouts could find him.

"Ray Charles could see he was a great player," said Dubenion, the former Bills' receiver who at the time was working as a scout for Buffalo. "He was fast, caught the ball in traffic, he was just great. It didn't matter what level he came from, he could play."

Dubenion has spent a long time scouting players for a variety of teams, but Reed remains his most-prized catch. During 15 magnificent years in Buffalo Reed caught 941 passes for 13,095 yards and 86 touchdowns, numbers that could someday grant him residence in the Pro Football Hall of Fame.

"Andre Reed is right up there," former Bills' receivers coach Charlie Joiner said a few years ago. "You have to consider Andre as one of the best because he's done it for a lot of years, and he's

been consistent."

Reed made a living going over the middle to catch Jim Kelly passes, and then what set him apart from most of his contemporaries was that he would make a move or break a tackle to pile up the ultra-valuable yards after the catch.

Reed was never considered a speed burner because he didn't have that top end 40-yard dash burst like Don Beebe, but he had terrific game speed, and when defensive backs overlooked that facet, that's when Reed was his most dangerous.

And one other thing. He was a gamer.

"That'll be my legacy," Reed said. "I know every time I went out on the field, I tried to do my best, and I came to play. When the chips were down and we needed a big play, I could always be called on, I could always make a play. Not too many guys can say they did that."

It all began on the series following McDowell's interception.

The Bills took possession at the 50 after Al Del Greco's squib kick caromed off Mark Maddox who then picked up the ball and returned it 15 yards. Ten plays later, Kenneth Davis – playing for Thurman Thomas who was knocked out of the game just before McDowell's interception with a hip pointer – plunged over from the one to make it 35-10.

"We took it in there and scored and it wasn't that hard, so maybe they (the Oilers) did relax some," center Kent Hull said. Christie then successfully recovered his own onside kick at the Buffalo 48 and 56 seconds later, Reich, who finished 21-of-34 for 289 yards and four TDs, lofted a 38-yard touchdown pass to Don Beebe.

"I thought the onside kickoff we recovered was huge and at that point the momentum turned our way," Hull said.

Said Reich: "The onside kick was a big momentum shift. That was definitely a turning point, but when you're down that much, the defense still had to make some big plays."

It did. The Oilers went three and out and a poor 25-yard Greg Montgomery punt gave the Bills the ball at their own 41. Four plays later Reich threaded a perfect strike to Reed over the middle for a 26-yard touchdown and suddenly, it was 35-24.

The fans – those who hadn't left and were trying to get back into the stadium – were in an uproar. "I couldn't believe that noise, I've never heard our crowd so loud," Hull said.

"When we scored to make it 35-24 late in the third quarter, that's when I thought it was really within reach," Reich said. "If the defense just kept playing the way they were playing and the offense kept executing, there was plenty of time."

Sure enough, the defense continued it's miraculous recovery as Henry Jones picked off a Moon pass and brought it back to the Houston 23. After two Davis runs for five yards and an incompletion, the Bills were faced with fourth-and-five. Following a timeout, coach Marv Levy eschewed the field goal and the bold move paid off as Reich fired a perfect strike to Reed in the end zone to make it 35-31.

"I told the other coaches if we hit a fourth, we're going for it," Levy said. "The reasoning was if we make the field goal, we're still down by eight."

After an exchange of punts, Houston drove from its own 10 to the Buffalo 14. However, the Bills kept the Oilers out of the end zone and their hard work paid off when Montgomery, Houston's holder on placekicks, dropped the snap on a field goal attempt and the Bills took over at the 26. Within seven plays – one a 35-yard Davis run on third-and-four – Reich and Reed hooked up for the third straight time, this one a 17-yard score, and the Bills were ahead, 38-35, with 3:08 remaining.

"This is very emotional for me," Reed said. "The last half of the year I really haven't been in the offense and today they were calling my number and trying to get me the ball. It feels good to be back where I usually am. Good things come to those who wait and I've been waiting a long time this year, a half a season, so I'm glad it happened today. I don't think anything changed, I think it was just a matter of throwing me the ball, period. You have to take your hat off to Frank, he tried to find me and he did."

The Oilers managed to force overtime when Moon – who completed a then NFL playoff-record 36 passes for a Houston playoff-record 371 yards – marched them 63 yards to set up Del Greco's tying 26-yard field goal with 12 seconds left.

Buffalo lost the coin toss to start the extra period, but that wound up working in its favor because on the third play of OT Nate Odomes intercepted a poorly thrown Moon pass and returned it to the Oilers 20. After two Davis plunges, Christie came on and kicked the game-winning field goal to complete what Houston cornerback Cris Dishman termed not the greatest comeback in history, but the "biggest choke in history."

Long after the celebration on the field spilled back into the locker room, the Bills were still shaking their heads in disbelief. "I have to admit, it's a tremendous thrill to be a part of a game like this," Levy said. "They don't happen often."

Nose tackle Jeff Wright summed up both teams' amazement over what transpired this way: "I went up to Ray Childress and he said to me 'I've never seen anything like this' and his eyes were like bugged out. I told him 'Me either.' I've never witnessed anything like this, it was a great win."

The next day it was business as usual for Levy. "It was great to win, it was very exhilarating, it was exciting, but it's over and we're plunged in to our Pittsburgh preparations," he said nonchalantly. "That's the problem with coaching or playing, you can't celebrate too long. It was a great feeling last night and early this morning around the coffee machine, but we're back to work." And that work paid off. With Reich at quarterback the Bills defeated the Steelers at Three Rivers Stadium, and then with Kelly back at the helm, the Bills traveled to Miami and whipped the Dolphins in the AFC Championship Game. However, the season crashed to an end for the third year in a row when Dallas embarrassed the Bills 52-17 in Super Bowl 27.

April 24, 1993 – Buffalo, N.Y.
Memorial Auditorium

May Day

"May day, May day, May day" Rick Jeanneret screamed from the press box high above the ice surface at Memorial Auditorium the night Brad May brought an end to 10 years of first-round flopping by the Sabres. Not since 1983 had the Sabres advanced out of the opening round of the NHL playoffs, but when May scored in overtime to win Game 4 and complete Buffalo's four-game sweep of the rival Boston Bruins, the explosion of emotion from the fans nearly imploded the Aud.

As they waited anxiously to skate back onto the Memorial Auditorium ice for the start of overtime, there was a surge of bravado coursing through the Buffalo Sabres locker room.

Someone shouted that he was going to score the game-winning goal against the hated Boston Bruins. Then someone else refuted that testimonial and said, no, he was going to score the winner. And then someone else chimed in, and someone else, and someone else.

"A lot of guys were saying 'I got it, I got it, I want to beat these guys,'" defenseman Doug Bodger said.

Sure it was the confidence of youth, but it was also a case of these young Sabres sensing the moment and understanding what was at stake. This was not going to be just any goal. Whoever scored this goal would reserve a permanent and prominent place for himself in Sabres' lore, forever to be known as the man who not only completed a delicious four-game sweep of the Bruins, but also the man who exorcised the dastardly demons of playoffs past for the Sabres.

Not surprisingly, second-year Sabre Brad May wasn't making any predictions. And if he had dared to stand up, pound his chest and proclaim himself ready to score the goal that would end Buffalo's mysterious and miserable run of first-round playoff disappointment which dated to 1984, his teammates probably would have looked at him en masse and said "Yeah, right."

You see, May hadn't exactly been on a tear of late. He had gone the final 27 regular-season games without a goal, and now, three games and three periods into this impossible-to-figure series in which Buffalo held a stunning three games to none lead over the heavily-favored Bruins, his drought dragged on. Never mind scoring; May had managed just one shot on goal to this point. One shot.

Suffice it to say that Las Vegas wouldn't have given you odds on May. He had about as much chance of scoring as the Rigas family has of saving face in Western New York.

"Hey, I had to come around sometime," May said.

What a time to come around. At 4:48 of the overtime May sliced his way through center ice, took a pass from Pat LaFontaine, outmaneuvered future Hall of Fame defenseman Ray Bourque, then threw a beautiful deke on goaltender Andy Moog before wristing the puck into the net to bring an unforgettably dramatic conclusion to the game, the series, and the first-round floundering.

The Aud erupted into an ear-splitting cacophony of celebration, brooms were flung onto the ice signifying the sweep, Sabre sticks and gloves flew like confetti, and up in the press box broadcaster Rick Jeanneret was spontaneously screaming "May Day, May Day, May Day," one of the great calls not only in team history, but hockey history.

In its previous seven trips to the playoffs the Sabres had failed to advance out of the first round each time, their record in those seven series a putrid 12-26. They had played the Bruins five times in their postseason history and had never defeated their arch rivals from Boston, twice losing heartbreaking seven-game epics, one of those coming the year before.

And there was no reason to believe the tide was about to turn. In analyzing this series before its beginning, no one with their sanity intact would have given the Sabres any chance of winning, let alone sweeping. Boston had closed the regular season winning eight games in a row to finish first in the Adams Division with 109 points. Buffalo had lost its last seven games to limp into the postseason with 86 points and a history of playoff failure weighing it down like an anchor. Although Alexander Mogilny had shattered the team record for goals in a season with 76, tying him for the fifth-highest single-season total in NHL history, and LaFontaine had set new club

(Bill Wippert)

After Brad May scored the biggest goal of his career, an overtime game-winner that capped the Sabres sweep of the Boston Bruins in the first round of the 1993 NHL playoffs, he skated back onto the Memorial Auditorium ice carrying a symbolic broom in his hands.

standards for assists (95) and points (148, second-best in the league behind Mario Lemieux), this was Boston's series to win.

Instead, it became Buffalo's to win, and the Sabres did.

"I don't know," Bruins general manager Harry Sinden said when asked to explain how this could have happened. "Maybe it would be better to do nothing like the Sabres all year, then do well in the playoffs." Was that sarcasm or jealousy dripping from the corners of Sinden's mouth?

Sabres coach John Muckler chose to spin it another way. Following the Sabres' 7-4 regular-season-ending loss to Philadelphia, its seventh defeat in a row which tied a club futility mark dating back to the inaugural year of the franchise in 1970, Muckler said of the upcoming series with Boston, "They're due for a loss and we're due for a win."

And so it began. After blowing leads of 2-0 and 4-2 in Game 1 at Boston Garden, the Sabres pulled it out when Bob Sweeney – who had been waived by the Bruins

before the season and picked up by Buffalo – scored 11:03 into overtime. Cam Neely and Steve Heinze had scored for Boston in the final 4:16 of regulation against Grant Fuhr to force the extra period, but Sweeney produced what he called "The biggest goal of my career. It's poetic justice."

The Sabres were poetry in motion in Game 2 as Fuhr – looking like the five-time Stanley Cup-winning goalie from his days in Edmonton – turned aside 34 shots while Wayne Presley, Randy Wood, Mogilny and Dale Hawerchuk scored in a startling 4-0 victory. "We won the first game in Boston Garden last year and we felt that was satisfactory and it cost us in the series," Wood said. "This year the guys drew on that experience. We weren't satisfied with a split. We came out to pursue a sweep."

He was speaking of the two games in Boston. Mission accomplished, and now the Sabres set their

(Bill Wippert)

Pat LaFontaine drew an assist on the famous "May Day" goal which certainly wasn't a shock. During the 1992-93 season LaFontaine set numerous Sabres scoring records including most points (148) and most assists (95) in a single season.

heights a bit higher when the teams relocated to Buffalo for games 3 and 4: The pursuit of a series sweep. Just as they did in Game 1, the Sabres bolted to a 2-0 lead in Game 3, saw Boston rally to force overtime, then won it 1:05 into the extra session, this time on a power-play goal by Yuri Khmylev after Bourque had been forced to take down Bodger

PAT LAFONTAINE

It is reasonably safe to say that no professional athlete in Buffalo sports history has ever had a greater impact on his team and the community in a shorter time period than LaFontaine.

LaFontaine came to Buffalo in a trade from the New York Islanders prior to the 1991-92 season, but due to a knee injury and recurring concussions, he only played one full year (1992-93) of the six he was here. That year alone was enough to cement his legacy, though, as he finished second in the NHL in scoring behind Mario Lemieux with a team-record 148 points, the most ever scored by an American-born player, with many of the assists coming on goals by Alexander Mogilny who scored a team-record 76.

Every other year LaFontaine was a member of the Sabres, he missed huge chunks of playing time because of injury. Combining the 1993-94, 1994-95 and 1996-97 seasons, he played a total of just 51 games, and in 1997, when the Sabres refused to let him play because of his head injuries, they traded him – and his hefty salary – to the New York Rangers. His lone season with the Rangers was cut short by another concussion, and that's when he decided to retire for good.

"I've always said the most important thing is my wife and three children, and if it got to the point where I was above minimal risk, I would stop playing hockey," LaFontaine said the day he bid farewell to the game.

At the time of his retirement LaFontaine ranked second all-time to Joey Mullen in goals scored by an American (468) and third in points (1,013) behind Mullen and ex-Sabre Phil Housley.

Though he spent his first eight NHL seasons with the Islanders, his time in Buffalo was his most rewarding. He became captain of the team, and he became a pillar in the community as he served as a spokesperson for The United Way and was on the Board of Trustees for Children's Hospital.

For all the entertainment he provided Sabres fans on the ice when he was able to play, he has said on numerous occasions that he received equal gratification from Western New Yorkers. He once said that Buffalo would always be special to him "because of the people and inspiration I found here. Some special children I had met through the United Way and Children's Hospital inspired me through their courage (when he was battling post-concussion syndrome). To this day, they still inspire me. We talk about heroes, but people like that show us what courage and perseverance are all about."

who was streaking in on a breakaway.

Through an interpreter, Khmylev said "I've heard since I first got here that the Sabres have always gotten knocked out in the first round. I'm familiar with the history. I know the importance of the last goal."

He only wishes he could have scored it in Game 4, but that honor fell to May.

The game was played on an unseasonably balmy spring night in Buffalo, but that was nothing compared to the temperature in the Aud, a white-hot mixture of excitement and nervousness. The Sabres were on the brink of shocking the hockey world, but there was still the matter of their ignominious playoff history. "This is going to be the hardest one to win," Fuhr correctly predicted.

As expected, Boston came out determined to put off summer vacation at least another few days. Fuhr was strafed for four first-period goals before leaving with a strained knee, giving way to his backup, a 28-year-old Czech named Dominik Hasek. Mogilny and Hawerchuk scored for Buffalo in the first, but when Dave Poulin beat Hasek 2:13 into the second while the Bruins were short-handed for a 5-2 lead, it looked like a return trip to Boston was in the offing.

However, Donald Audette quickly answered Poulin, a key moment according to LaFontaine. "That third goal was huge," he said. "By getting that third goal we might have had them take a back seat. We always say a two-goal lead is the worst thing going into the third period."

It was. Midway through the third the Sabres scored twice within 53 seconds to tie the game at 5-5. Mogilny unleashed a slapshot from near the left faceoff circle that blew through Moog's legs, and then Hawerchuk dug a puck out behind the net and fed Khmylev who flicked a wrist shot past Moog's glove.

On to overtime where Hasek gave May the chance to be the hero, making two tough saves early in the period, a pre-cursor of what was to come from Hasek over the next eight years. The tension was building and the fans were close to the breaking point, dying to let loose all those years of frustration.

And then in a flash it was over. Keith Carney slid the puck up to LaFontaine who was knocked down but maintained control, and on his knees swept the puck in the direction of May. May found himself one-on-one with Bourque, one of the best to ever play the game. In this rarest of instances, though, Bourque wasn't up to the challenge as May faked him out. "I saw (Bourque) coming out of the corner of my eye," May recalled. "It's something that 99 times out of 100 isn't going to work, especially against Ray Bourque. He probably didn't expect (the move) from someone like myself."

With Bourque in his wake, all that was left was Moog. May thought of shooting quickly, but instead made a couple moves that drew Moog out of position and with an open net yawning at him, May didn't miss.

LaFontaine couldn't have done it better himself. "What a goal," said the author of 53 goals during the regular season compared to May's 13. "It was just fake, fake, goal. What a great goal for Maysie, that's something he'll always remember."

It was something Sabres' fans will remember forever, too. "I'm happiest for the people of Buffalo right now," LaFontaine said. "I think they are probably letting out a lot of emotion they have held in for some time."

Unfortunately for the Sabres, that was the last game they would win that season. They ran into the Montreal Canadiens in the Adams Division finals and were swept out in four straight, each game ending 4-3 with two decided in overtime. Montreal then went on to defeat the Islanders in the conference finals, and Wayne Gretzky and his Los Angeles Kings in the Stanley Cup Finals behind goaltender Patrick Roy.

April 27, 1994 – Buffalo, N.Y.
Memorial Auditorium

Breakfast at the Aud

"It wasn't Dale Hawerchuk, it wasn't Alexander Mogilny, nor was it Donald Audette, Yuri Khmylev, Derek Plante and Randy Wood, the other Sabres who scored at least 20 goals during the 1993-94 regular season. No, the man who scored one of the most memorable goals in Sabres history, the goal in the fourth overtime period that ended Game 6 of the first-round playoff series between the Sabres and New Jersey Devils, the sixth-longest game in NHL history, was Dave Hannan. That's right, Dave Hannan.

When Dominik Hasek sat down in front of his locker, body dripping wet from a much-needed shower, one towel wrapped around his torso and another draped over his shoulders, he looked like a man who, well, had just taken a shower.

Throughout his extraordinary nine seasons in Buffalo, Hasek's impeccable physical fitness astounded his teammates perhaps as much as the acrobatic, eye-popping saves he routinely made on a nightly basis. But this was ridiculous.

All around him his Sabres teammates sat slumped in front of their lockers, paralyzed with exhaustion, straining to button their shirts or pull on their pants, and for good reason. They had just participated in the sixth-longest game in National Hockey League history, a six-hour, 12-minute marathon that ended at 1:52 a.m. when Buffalo's Dave Hannan mercifully backhanded a shot past New Jersey goalie Martin Brodeur 5:43 into the fourth overtime period at Memorial Auditorium for the only goal of the night, and morning.

Yet here was Hasek, resembling a man who had just competed in a strenuous game of Scrabble rather than the sixth game of an NHL playoff series where, for more than 65 minutes of stomach-churning overtime, one mistake would have brought an end to the Sabres' season. As he sat there surrounded by a horde of reporters, this freak of nature looked like he could play another three-plus overtime periods if need be.

"I haven't been sleeping well lately, but I slept for about three hours Wednesday afternoon and I felt good," Hasek said following a performance during which he stopped all 70 Devils shots – 39 of them in the overtime sessions – enabling the Sabres to ward off first-round elimination and extend the series to a deciding seventh game back in New Jersey two days hence.

Amazing what a three-hour nap can do for a world-class athlete. "Hasek played the best game I've ever seen a goaltender play," said New Jersey's Bobby Carpenter.

Added Brodeur, who stopped the first 49 shots he saw before Hannan finally beat him: "We had so many chances, but (Hasek) came up big. It was unbelievable."

Hasek did admit to a brief spell of languor during the second overtime. "But I think the other players were more tired than I was," he said. "The shots in overtime weren't so hard. They don't handle the puck so good (because they're fatigued) so it's easier for a goaltender."

The Sabres had finished the 1993-94 regular season fourth in the Northeast Division of the Eastern Conference with 95 points. They drew as their first-round opponent the Devils who had amassed 106 points in placing second behind the New York Rangers in the Atlantic Division, for a series matching the two best defensive teams in

(Bill Wippert)

Not known for his scoring touch, Dave Hannan was in the right place at the right time in the fourth overtime in Game Six of the 1994 first-round playoff series against New Jersey. Hannan backhanded the puck past Devils' goalie Martin Brodeur to end the longest Sabres' game in history.

the NHL.

With three victories in the four regular-season meetings, New Jersey was the consensus favorite, but the Sabres got the early jump as Hasek delivered a 30-save shutout to key a 2-0 victory in the series opener at the Meadowlands. New Jersey took games 2 and 3 by 2-1 scores, then Buffalo's offense finally showed up as Wayne Presley and Yuri Khymlev each scored twice and the Sabres won Game 4 at the Aud, 5-3.

Hasek's goals-against average through four games was a skinny 1.76 – even better than the 1.95 mark he compiled during the regular season, best in Sabres' history and enough to clinch his first Vezina Trophy. But the Devils owned him in Game 5. Buffalo grabbed a 3-1 lead five minutes into the second period only to see New Jersey score four unanswered goals to take a 5-3 victory, putting the Sabres on the brink of elimination as the teams headed back to Buffalo for what would become one of the epic games in NHL history.

"We don't want to have to come back here, we're going to try to end it up there," Devils defenseman Bruce Driver said following the Game 5 victory.

The Devils tried. They tried for more than six periods to send the Sabres into the offseason. The Sabres would have none of it. Hasek would have none of it. As for the officials? Hmmnn.

Three pucks found their way into the New Jersey net in Game 6, but only Hannan's was deemed a goal by referee Terry Gregson.

Midway through the second period defenseman Ken Sutton snapped a wrist shot past Brodeur, but the goal was disallowed when Gregson slapped Jason Dawe with a goaltender interference penalty. Replays showed Dawe being ridden into Brodeur by the crafty Claude Lemieux, but Gregson ruled against Buffalo.

About five minutes later, Brodeur stopped a shot by Dale Hawerchuk and when Presley crashed the net looking for a rebound the puck struck his left skate and creeped across the goal line. At first Gregson signaled a goal, but after looking at the replay he changed his mind, saying Presley kicked at the puck. Play was delayed five minutes after many in the crowd of 15,003 littered the ice in protest.

"Honestly, I didn't even know where the puck was until the light went on," said Presley. "They thought I kicked it into the net, but I didn't. If they thought I could move my feet like that, I should play soccer."

Said Sabres coach John Muckler: "I guess you stay focused because you're playing for your life, but I didn't think those goals should have been waved off. This was a great game, but it probably should have never gotten to this point."

He's right, because even without the controversial non-goals, this game wouldn't have gone beyond regulation if not for a simply stunning save Hasek made on Stephane Richer in the third period. Bobby Holik picked up a loose puck in the neutral zone and came in 2-on-1 with Richer. Holik passed across the slot and Richer had the entire left side of the net to shoot at, but Hasek leaped across, did a gymnast's split, and kicked the shot out with his leg pad.

"He waited for a while because the pass was not easy for him and I could make a move," Hasek said of Richer. "All their best shooters are right-handed. I knew that's a save I might have to make, so I worked on it yesterday in practice."

DAVE HANNAN

Dale Hawerchuk was the No. 1 pick in the 1981 NHL Entry Draft by the Winnipeg Jets. The Pittsburgh Penguins waited until the 10th round, with the 196th overall pick, to select gritty winger Dave Hannan that year.

Hawerchuk and his 518 goals and 1,409 points are enshrined in the Hockey Hall of Fame while Hannan and his 114 goals and 305 points will only be a visitor to the museum in downtown Toronto.

But during the fourth overtime period of Game 6 of the Buffalo-New Jersey playoff series in 1994, it was Hannan, not Hawerchuk – or for that matter Alexander Mogilny – who scored one of the most memorable goals in NHL history.

"I've always been a big part of a team's success in a small way," said Hannan, alluding to the fact that he was the type of player who did the little things that are so vital in the winning of hockey games, but rarely did he do the big things, like scoring overtime goals in the playoffs.

"And that's what makes me feel good," Hannan continued, "because I've always been consistent and the respect of my teammates is what I enjoy. That is what you look for in the game."

He sure earned a measure of respect that night, not to mention hearty thank yous all around from his exhausted teammates after he ended the sixth-longest game in NHL history.

"I've played a long time, I have a lot of great memories, but this is special," he said. "A guy like me who has been a defensive player most of his career, to score a goal like that and get some nice accolades was fun. I don't score a lot so I was kidding the guys. I said 'Guys, whoever scores might have a free ticket to the Hall of Fame.'"

He won't go to the Hall of Fame. But it was certainly a Hall of Fame type goal.

So on to the first overtime they went, during which each team killed off a penalty to preserve the tie. And then to a second overtime, where Carpenter missed an open net with a one-timer, and Hawerchuk clanged one off the post. And then to a third overtime where the Devils carried the play and out-shot the Sabres, 14-5, to no avail. And then to a fourth overtime, where Hasek made three difficult stops, allowing Hannan to become the hero.

Slowly but surely the Aud began to thin out as the evening dragged on and Wednesday night morphed into Thursday morning. Many fans, anxious to see an outcome but wary of the clock and an early-morning wakeup call for work or school, filed out, but more than half of the original crowd was still there at the end.

"I thought they were great hanging in here that long," Sabres defenseman Randy Moller said of the fans who stayed. "And they were still yelling and screaming at the end. Maybe they passed out amphetamines or something."

No drugs, but one of the fans, or survivors, had a pretty good idea. "They should have passed out pillows and blankets and started making pancakes," he told a reporter from *The Buffalo News*.

The guy up in the press box responsible for playing music between play stoppages elicited some weary smiles from the fans with a number of appropriate selections including *"A Hard Day's Night," "Rock Around the Clock," "We Gotta Get Out of This Place," "After Midnight"* and *"One is the Loneliest Number."*

And even the players made light of the situation. "Going out for the seventh period," Sabres winger Randy Wood recalled, "guys in the locker room were saying 'This is unbelievable. Somebody score a goal. We've got to go home, we're going to have a huge babysitting bill.'"

That it was Hannan who scored the goal that cut into those babysitters' profits came as a surprise given that he was a defensive forward who had scored just six goals in 83 games that season. Then again, it was no surprise at all.

"It's funny, they say in overtime games in the playoffs, it's the grinders who always score the goal," Hannan said. "Our line (he, Presley and Dawe) had a lot of chances to score that night. A couple of times, Wayne and I came down on two-on-ones. I didn't want to shoot, so I passed it over to him and let him take the shot because he's the scorer on our line. He would come back to the bench {after not scoring} and say, `Just shoot the puck. If you get a chance, just shoot the puck.'"

So Hannan took his linemate's advice and scored the goal that permanently attached his name to NHL lore.

"The goal was just an innocent play where Dawe forechecked well behind the net," Hannan recalled. "Presley went straight for the net and took out the defenseman, and then I cruised in behind him looking for the loose puck. It went right to my backhand, and I just shot it as quickly as I could. Then, wham! In it goes and my first thoughts are, `We're going to Game 7.' Then I was so tired I wanted to lie down right there."

Brodeur remembered the sequence this way: "The guy from the corner (Dawe) made a one-handed pass in front. I went down for it, it hit a stick or something and the guy (Hannan) went across the grain. He roofed it up there, he made a good shot. I was thinking 'I hope he's going to miss the puck or somebody is going to hit him or something.'"

Nobody hit Hannan, probably because nobody could. "I was so tired I don't remember what was going on," said New Jersey defenseman Tommy Albelin, who tried to whack the puck out of harm's way, but fanned.

Muckler recalled being so impressed with the way Hannan played because it was a typical Hannan game. "He probably did more valuable things before he scored the goal than when he actually scored it," Muckler said. "He killed penalties that night and gave us a chance to win. He kept his poise and when he got the opportunity to score, he did."

Muckler quipped afterward that "I just thought we played a doubleheader so we should have gotten credit for two wins and win the series." Too bad it didn't work that way because two nights later, the Sabres lost the seventh game at the Meadowlands, 2-1. They were thoroughly outplayed, and only Hasek's brilliance kept them in the game as he made 44 saves while Brodeur was asked to make just 17, though his last save was his best, a spectacular robbery of Hawerchuk with 16 seconds remaining that preserved New Jersey's victory. While the Sabres headed out to the golf course, the Devils went on to defeat Boston in six games, then lost to the eventual Stanley Cup champion New York Rangers in seven magnificent games, the finale going to double overtime. As wonderful a memory as his game-winning goal was, Hannan remembers almost as vividly a near-miss in Game 7, a goal that perhaps could have led to a series victory for the Sabres. "I had a shot in Game 7 that I put right into (Brodeur's) glove," Hannan said. "Had that one gone in, who knows, the series was that close. Let's face it, they beat us. They were the better team, but it was really close. The series had everything – good hockey, good hitting, coaching, great goaltending. Even now people say it may have been one of the best series they ever saw."

April 29, 1997 – Buffalo, N.Y.
Marine Midland Arena

Planting One on Ottawa

*Marine Midland Arena, now known as HSBC Arena, officially became a place of
Buffalo sporting worship the night the Sabres defeated the Ottawa Senators in
Game 7 of their 1997 first-round playoff series. The shiny new building was nothing
more than a place to watch hockey – devoid of the memories that still stirred a
couple blocks away at vacant Memorial Auditorium. But then Derek Plante's slap
shot in overtime blew through Ottawa goaltender Ron Tugnutt and trickled ever so
slowly across the goal line to give the Sabres the victory and the new place a
memory of its own to cherish a lifetime.*

For as wonderful a scene as it was on the ice, his young Buffalo Sabre teammates gid-
dily celebrating one of the franchise's greatest victories, veteran defenseman Garry
Galley knew the best was yet to come.

So after spending a few minutes partaking in the revelry that followed Derek
Plante's never-to-be-forgotten overtime goal which decided Game 7 of Buffalo's 1997
first-round playoff series against the Ottawa Senators at Marine Midland Arena, Galley
scrambled back to the locker room and grabbed a prime seat for the show.

"I watched everyone come in," he said. "I was one of the first guys in the room. I
saw Teddy (Nolan, the head coach), Paul (Theriault, assistant coach), Donny (Lever,
assistant coach) and all of the players. I really got a jolt out of watching those guys
come in with their smiles. I knew what they were feeling, because I had been there
before. To see these guys have that kind of smile on their faces after seeing so many
long faces through this series over a lot of things, I think it was nice.

"A lot of the guys hadn't experienced this. It's something you cannot put into
words. You cannot teach it. For them to feel it and be a part of it is something that will
help this organization take a real step forward."

Galley will never forget those priceless Kodak moments, those snapshots of gap-
toothed Sabre kids like Plante and Michael Peca and Matthew Barnaby and Steve
Shields bouncing into the locker room in the aftermath of this pulsating 3-2 victory that
brought an end to a tumultuous and fabulously exciting NHL Eastern Conference playoff quarterfinal series.

And none of the 18,595 patrons in the building that night will ever forget the
sight of Plante's hot slap shot burning a hole through Ottawa goalie Ron Tugnutt's glove,
the puck seemingly moving in slow motion as it floated into the net with Tugnutt unable
to reach behind him to keep it out.

There hasn't been much history written at the seven-year-old downtown barn,
which now goes by the moniker HSBC Arena, but on this night the first chapter was

crafted as the Sabres' victory enabled them to advance to the second round of the play-offs for just the second time since 1983.

"This is something you dream of as a kid growing up," said Buffalo tough guy Rob Ray, who had endured more playoff heartbreak in Buffalo than anyone else in the room. "In the eight years I've been here this is just the second time we've been able to do this. I just hope we can continue this. All the controversies that we've had to put behind us, we wanted to do it for ourselves, for the guys in this locker room. It was a personal vendetta to go out there and do our best."

No one did better than Plante. He was credited with the tying goal in the third period, and then delivered the winner that produced the loudest roar heard in Buffalo since *New York Daily News* columnist Mike Lupica tagged the Buffalo Bills "the serial killers of the Super Bowl" a few years earlier.

"What do I feel?" Plante said. "Relief. It's over and we're finally going on. There's been so much talk about how we haven't been able to get past the first round. We did it."

This was the Sabres first Game 7 appearance at home in their history and their first victory in a Game 7 after three previous losses. Also, it was just their second series

(Bill Wippert)

This goal by Derek Plante, which Ottawa goalie Ron Tugnutt got a piece of but couldn't handle, gave the Sabres a 3-2 victory over the Senators in Game Seven of their first-round playoff series in 1997, the first big moment in the brief life of the new downtown arena.

triumph in their last 12 dating to the 1982-83 season.

"You can't look at the past, the guys that are here now are the guys that have to look to the future," said Brian Holzinger, who assisted on Buffalo's first goal of the game by Donald Audette.

Said Ray: "If we didn't win the first round, everybody would have remembered all the negative stuff. Now we can go through and someone will have something to remember us by."

The Sabres got off to what could only be described as a brutal start. The Senators turned the Buffalo zone into a shooting gallery during the first period, pouring 11 shots on Steve Shields, with at least six of them quality scoring chances.

Thankfully, Shields was equal to the challenge and he allowed only one goal when Shawn McEachern nudged a rebound under his sprawled body during a Senators power play. The young goaltender was making his fourth consecutive start in the series after superstar Dominik Hasek had suffered a season-ending knee injury early in Game 3 at Ottawa. If not for Shields' early heroics, Plante would have never had a chance to produce his own.

"This is about as gutsy an effort as you're going to see," Dixon Ward said of Shields. "He just came out of nowhere. Nobody gave him much of a chance to contribute. When Dominik went down, a lot of people said, 'Oh, oh, trouble.' But he absolutely rose to the occasion. He is our series MVP."

After setting a playoff franchise record for fewest shots in a period (two), Buffalo remained in an offensive coma for most of the second period and had only eight shots through 36 minutes, but shot No. 9 finally found its way past Tugnutt.

With the Sabres on a

(Bill Wippert)

Rob Ray served as the Sabres enforcer from 1989 until late in the 2002-03 season, and he became one of the most popular players in team history.

power play, Galley sent the puck out to the blue line to Holzinger who fired a slap shot that Tugnutt stopped, but Audette was parked on the edge of the crease and stuffed the

ROB RAY

It was the evening of March 11, 2003, and on all the sports highlight shows, there was a clip of the newest Ottawa Senator doing what he had been doing his entire career – taking a penalty. For Rob Ray, those two minutes he was assessed for interference gave him 3,191 career penalty minutes, fifth-most in NHL history. Incredibly, his first 3,189 penalty minutes were earned during his career with the Sabres, most in history by one player on one team.

It was a strange sight that night watching Ray battle the Boston Bruins in the uniform of the Senators, but it was a stark reminder of the Sabres' financial plight. The day before, Ray's 13 1/2-year Buffalo career ended when Sabres general manager Darcy Regier traded Ray to Ottawa for future considerations.

Regier was looking to trim payroll from a team that barely had a payroll, but he also wanted to give Ray – who was likely going to retire at season's end – one last shot to win a Stanley Cup. "They didn't have to do it, and I appreciate that they did it," Ray said.

It was the least the Sabres could do. Ray played 889 games with Buffalo,

fourth-most in team history. He scored only 40 goals and 50 assists for 90 points, but his job was never about scoring. From the time he came up to the Sabres in the 1988-89 season, Ray was Buffalo's hammer, its enforcer. Whenever the team needed its dirty work done, Ray was sent over the boards to do it, and he did it proudly, effectively and sometimes bloodily.

"It's a thankless job night after night," said former Sabres captain Stu Barnes, who was traded the same day as Ray to the Dallas Stars. "He doesn't get to play a lot of minutes or score goals, but he has a very difficult job to do and he does it night after night. He's a character in the (locker) room, he's a great leader, and he cares very much not only about how the team is doing and the franchise, but he cares about things in the community."

Ray's impact in Buffalo was profound off the ice as well. He was always active in charitable work, and on the day he left town, he vowed to continue those endeavors. "My home is here, I'm not going anywhere," he said. "I'm just going out of town to work for a little while, but this is where I live."

rebound through the goalie's legs.

Ottawa recaptured a 2-1 lead 45 seconds into the third period when Wade Redden's seemingly harmless wrist shot from 45 feet ticked off Holzinger and sailed over Shields' left shoulder. However, the Sabres dominated the rest of the period with their best offensive pressure of the series and they managed to tie the game with a fluke goal of their own.

Plante won a faceoff from Alexei Yashin to the left of Tugnutt, the puck popped into the air and it floated right over Tugnutt's shoulder at 6:27. "I was actually trying to go to the net and was going to try to chip it by him and try to pass to (Michal) Grosek going to the net," Plante said. "Yashin realized it and he flung it harder than I did right into the net."

The Sabres carried play the rest of the period and brought the momentum into the overtime, but Ottawa had the better chances and Shields had to make two difficult saves to keep the Sabres alive. Then Plante turned a rather innocent looking play into a seismic occurrence when he knocked down a clearing attempt by Ottawa defenseman Steve Duchesne and unleashed a wicked drive that Tugnutt couldn't handle.

"As soon as he shot it, I kind of felt like it was going in," Nolan said. "To see the way it did go in, it kind of went in slow motion."

Said Plante: "Duchesne hit me in the chest coming through the neutral zone and I came down and I knew we had an odd man rush. I just took a stride and blasted it. It hit him (Tugnutt) and it went in. I saw him kind of dive back for it and the crowd erupted so that's when I knew it was in."

And thus, the Sabres, who had become known that year as the hardest working team in hockey, lived to work another few nights.

But only a few. Philadelphia quickly brought the Sabres back down to earth, winning the first three games of the Eastern Conference semifinals by scores of 5-3, 2-1 and 4-1, as Shields continued to play in place of Hasek. Buffalo's Ed Ronan won Game 4 in overtime to avert the sweep, but the Flyers returned to Buffalo and wrapped it up with a 6-3 victory. But this proved to be a useful learning experience for these young Sabres. The following year they advanced one round further to the Conference finals before bowing to Washington, and then in 1999, they made a dramatic run to the Stanley Cup Finals and gave an obviously more talented Dallas team a serious scare before falling in triple overtime in Game 6.

June 19, 1999 – Buffalo, N.Y.
Marine Midland Arena

No Goal

Brett Hull's skate was in the crease. He didn't deny it the night he scored one of the most controversial goals in NHL playoff history, and he doesn't deny it today. His skate was in the crease and he knew it, NHL commissioner Gary Bettman knew it, and all of Buffalo certainly knew it, but it doesn't matter. All that matters is that in the third overtime of Game 6 of the 1999 Stanley Cup Finals at Marine Midland Arena, Hull scored the game-winning, Cup-winning goal with his skate illegally in the crease, and the NHL officials egregiously allowed the goal to stand, ending the Sabres' glorious run that year in tumult and tears.

$\mathbf{A}$s Mike Modano stood amidst the bedlam that engulfed the Dallas Stars' locker room, he wore the same crooked grin a 4-year-old boy gives his mother when he's just done something naughty.

With champagne corks popping and the bubbly being sprayed all around him creating a Niagara Falls-type mist, Modano was asked to give his opinion of the Stanley Cup-winning goal scored by his linemate, Brett Hull, 14:51 into the third overtime period of Game 6.

Was Hull's skate in the goal crease when he pumped the puck past Buffalo's Dominik Hasek, ending the second-longest game in Finals history and touching off a controversy that still brews today in Buffalo?

"I saw it, and it looked like he did," Modano said. "But what can you do, drag us back out there and play?"

In other words, sorry Buffalo.

"I don't think I'm going to get dressed again and play," said Stars center Guy Carbonneau, echoing Modano's response 30 minutes after the issue – despite TV replays that clearly indicated Hull's skate was in the crease – had been decided in Dallas' favor. "What's done is done. If there's a controversy, that's too bad. I'm sorry about it, and I'm sure (the Sabres) are going to be upset, but for me, the season is over, the Cup is on our side and that's all that matters."

If only it were that simple. Originally instituted to help clear traffic in the crease, thus allowing goaltenders a fair opportunity to do their job while reducing the risk of injury, the in-the-crease rule had been a hot topic of debate for two years, mainly because too many goals were being disallowed, more than 100 in the 1998-99 season alone.

There should have been one more added to the list.

"If there's a guy in the crease before the puck goes in there, the goal doesn't count. It has happened all season long," said defenseman Jay McKee. "We're not whining, that's the rule. To have it end that way is devastating for us."

Rule 78-B states: "Unless the puck is in the goal crease area, a player of the attacking side may not enter nor stand in the goal crease. If a player has entered the crease prior to the puck and subsequently the puck should enter the net while such conditions prevail, the apparent goal shall not be allowed."

In this case, Hull took a shot from just outside the crease that Hasek stopped. The puck came back out of the crease, but Hull's skate remained inside the powder blue-painted area when he regained control of the puck and fired it into the net past a sprawling Hasek.

It should have been a no-brainer. No goal. Instead, no one from the NHL used any brains.

"It was our worst nightmare," said Sabres coach Lindy Ruff. "Somebody should have called from upstairs and said 'This is not a goal.' All I wanted was a review. I wanted (NHL commissioner Gary) Bettman to answer the question of why this wasn't reviewed. He turned his back on me. It was almost as if he knew the goal was tainted.

(Buffalo Sabres)

Most NHL observers felt the Sabres were an average team with a great goaltender when they reached the Stanley Cup Finals in 1999. What was certainly true about that statement is that Dominik Hasek was the NHL's premier goaltender and while he didn't win the Cup for Buffalo, he did win the league MVP award.

You can't explain the feeling."

Bryan Lewis, the NHL's director of officials, said the play was reviewed up in the replay booth and it was determined that Hull had continuous possession of the puck and thus was allowed to have a skate in the crease.

"The debate here seems to be did he or did he not have possession and control," Lewis said. "Our words from upstairs in our view was that yes he did, he played the puck from his foot to his stick, shot and scored. The other component of the debate is does the puck change (possession) as a result of hitting the goalie on the glove. Our rules are very clear in terms of completion of play. A puck that rebounds off the goalie, the goalpost, or an opposing player, is not deemed to be a change of possession and therefore Hull would be deemed to be in possession and control of the puck and allowed to shoot and score a goal even though the one foot was in the crease in advance of the puck."

It was clear that wasn't what happened. There were two separate possessions, in between which Hull's skate entered the crease illegally.

No goal.

No goal.

No goal.

"I congratulate the Dallas Stars, they played well, but I'm very bitter because of what happened, to lose like that," said Hasek. "You play for two months and the video judge didn't do his job. I don't know what he was doing, he must have been sleeping. I can't imagine this. I didn't know he was in the crease right away, but then I saw the replay in the trainers room and I was about to go back on the ice because I couldn't believe it."

Sabres captain Michael Peca floated the theory that once the Stars began their celebration, the NHL decided it was too late to right the wrong.

"It's a case where they didn't have the nerve after all the celebration to call the goal back," he said. "What can you do? It's over and I guess it will be a story for a long time."

It was the cruelest of endings for the Sabres, a bitter and polemical loss in a game that, by all rights, they really should have won. But in the end, the same problem that plagued Buffalo for most of the regular season – difficulty scoring goals – proved to be its undoing.

The Sabres set a new Finals record for fewest goals scored in a six-game series with nine, and even worse, this six-game series actually lasted nearly 22 periods. The old mark had been 11 goals by the Toronto Maple Leafs during their 1940 loss to the New York Rangers.

During the regular season, the Sabres' 207 goals ranked 16th in the 27-team NHL, but it was only four goals more than Buffalo's lowest total ever, 203 set in 1971-72, the franchise's second year of existence.

The Sabres fired 54 shots at Dallas goalie Ed Belfour, but only Stu Barnes' wrister in the second period found the mark. In the final 10 periods of the series, that was the only goal Belfour and the stout Dallas defense allowed.

"Obviously it's something we fought a lot of the year," Peca said of the goal shortage. "But don't forget we were playing Dallas six times in a row. It's a team that can really frustrate you. We thought we did a great job in creating chances, but Belfour played outstanding. At the end of the day, it's disappointing."

What was not disappointing was Buffalo's impressive display of guts, heart, passion and determination against a Dallas team that was clearly superior in terms of talent. "I said we'd play our best game of the series, and they gave it everything they had," said Ruff. "I thought we outplayed them. In the end it wasn't X's and O's that won them the game. We hit a post, we hit a crossbar, we couldn't buy a bounce."

The long, long, long night certainly started sourly for Buffalo. Despite being thoroughly dominated by the Dallas defense in a 2-0 Game 5 defeat back in Dallas which put the Stars in command of the series, the Sabres came out flying at Marine Midland Arena, buoyed by a ravenous, pom-pom-waving crowd. They tested Belfour early, but he was equal to the challenge.

Play was still tilted heavily in Buffalo's favor when, 8:09 into the opening period, Dallas' Jere Lehtinen scored a fluky goal that, like a pin plunging into a balloon let all the air out of the energized arena. Lehtinen,

(Buffalo Sabres)

Brett Hull hoisted the Stanley Cup for all of Buffalo to see, but Sabres fans couldn't see it through angry, misty eyes. Hull scored the Cup-winning goal in the third overtime of Game Six although it should not have counted because replays clearly showed his skate was illegally in the goal crease when he shot the puck past Dominik Hasek.

standing about 15 feet to Hasek's right, flipped a harmless looking shot that somehow found a crease between Hasek's hip and the near post. Hasek couldn't believe it. For that matter, neither could Lehtinen, but there it was: 1-0 Dallas, and now it was really going to be tough for the Sabres.

Once they had the lead the Stars settled into their familiar defensive shell which, at least in 1998-99, no team played better. The Stars frustrated the Sabres for the rest of the first period, and about half of the second, and it was starting to look like Lehtinen's goal might be enough to enable the Stars to skate back to the Sun Belt with the Stanley Cup.

But just after the Sabres killed off a Dallas power play during which Hasek made a couple of terrific saves, the momentum began to shift Buffalo's way, and it never really altered again. The Sabres attacked the Dallas net and peppered Belfour from every angle. He nearly withstood the entire barrage, but Barnes whipped a shot over his block-

---

MICHAEL PECA

In March 2002, when Peca played his first game at Buffalo's HSBC Arena since his trade from the Sabres to the New York Islanders the previous summer, he knew what to expect: Booing. Lots of booing. And that's what he got.

"I'd been hoping that people would reflect on the things I did for this organization and this community rather than how they viewed a contract negotiation," Peca said. "But that's the way it goes."

Every time Peca touched the puck that night he was voraciously serenaded, and the only cheer he drew was when he lost an edge and tumbled clumsily to the ice. Oh well, so much for that 'C' he wore on his Sabres sweater, and for the Selke Trophy he won in 1997 for being the NHL's best defensive forward, and for the leadership he provided during Buffalo's run to the Stanley Cup Finals in 1999.

Peca's Buffalo career was a short one, five years on the ice and one in limbo when he and the team's management couldn't come to a contract agreement, prompting him to sit out the entire 2000-01 season. In those five years he established a true connection with the fans of Buffalo who appreciated his blue-collar work ethic. But it all blew apart during his bitter contract squabble when he asked for what many fans thought was too much money and then refused to back down when the Sabres didn't meet his demand.

"I can't have any bad feelings toward the fans because they're part of the reason I enjoyed playing there so much," said Peca, who was finally traded to the Islanders for Tim Connolly and Taylor Pyatt.

It's just too bad that all the good things Peca did for the Sabres, he now does for the Islanders. And is it any surprise that since the trade, the Islanders, with Peca serving as captain, have enjoyed far more success than the Sabres?

---

er from about 25 feet out with 1:39 left in the second period to tie the game.

Wayne Primeau rushed into the Dallas end along the right boards with Barnes serving as his wing man. Barnes beat Carbonneau across the blue line and Primeau fed him neatly. Barnes got to the circle and whipped a shot over diving Dallas defenseman Craig Ludwig that beat Belfour and nestled into the upper far corner.

That goal sent a surge of electricity coursing throughout Western New York. The sellout crowd of 18,595 inside the arena nearly lifted the roof. More than 12,000 fans gathered down Washington Street rocked Dunn Tire Park as they watched on the JumboTron. And in every home and place of business where the television was tuned to ESPN, shouts of glee could be heard.

In the third period the Sabres continued to play with reckless abandon, and though they couldn't produce as many shots, the ones they did were quality chances. Joe Juneau had a shot just trickle wide of the post with 12:20 remaining in regulation, and Belfour made a nice pad save to stop a Miroslav Satan one-timer from the slot.

The Stars came out of their shell and made Hasek earn his keep, and the superstar played the way he's supposed to as he made all 10 saves he was called on to make and the game headed to overtime.

In the first extra period both teams played it close to the vest, afraid to make the critical mistake. But in the second overtime play opened up as both teams had numerous chances to end the game, none more glaring than Buffalo's James Patrick as he rang one off the cross bar at the 2:16 mark.

Into the third overtime they went, and despite battling exhaustion, both teams had a couple of great chances to win before Hull finally brought the curtain down on Buffalo's season.

There is no way to tell if the Sabres would have gone on to win even if the right call had been made on the Hull no-goal. But to have denied Buffalo that opportunity seemed criminal.

"I believe everybody will remember this as the Stanley Cup that was never won in 1999," said Juneau. "The goal was not a legal goal. I think because it was a goal that gave them the Stanley Cup, everybody jumped on the ice and they were afraid to make the call."

"It was such a great series, a great battle by both teams, and for it to be ended on a goal that shouldn't be counted, it doesn't make sense," said McKee. "First of all, to lose is devastating, but to lose on a call like that? I can't comprehend why our season is all of a sudden over."

What is also hard to comprehend is that four years removed from that night, the Sabres have gone from Stanley Cup runner-up to Stanley Cup pretender. A couple days after the loss, then Sabres' owner John Rigas announced at a parade in honor of the Sabres that he was going to "get the tools necessary to finish the job." Rigas did not follow up on that promise. Instead, he and his sons were arrested and jailed in the spring of 2002 as a result of the Adelphia Communications scandal which also helped drive the Sabres into bankruptcy.

January 8, 2000 – Nashville, Tenn.
Adelphia Coliseum

Music City Miracle

Wade Phillips admitted to having seen just about everything during his long coach-
ing career in the NFL, "But I haven't seen one like that," the ex-Bills coach said.
Neither had anyone else. In what ranks as one of the most galling defeats in Bills
history, Tennessee used a gadget play called Home Run Throwback – which includ-
ed a lateral that Bills fans remain convinced to this day was illegal – to return a
kickoff 75 yards for the winning touchdown with three seconds remaining in the
1999 AFC wild-card playoff game.

Six months had passed since the most disappointing and diabolical defeat of his career
– and for that matter, the career of every other member of the Buffalo Bills – yet it was
clear that the pain had not subsided for Marcellus Wiley.

When Buffalo's 2000 training camp commenced, the hangover from the Bills'
bizarre 22-16 wild-card playoff loss to Tennessee the previous January lingered unmis-
takably, nowhere more evident than in the face of the normally affable and free-smiling
Wiley.

"I've never been through that type of devastation as an athlete," Wiley recalled
with a somber expression when reporters asked him to re-live the memory of the Titans'
Home Run Throwup – er, Home Run Throwback – kickoff return in the waning seconds
that turned a glorious Buffalo victory into a never-to-be-forgotten loss.

Ditto for Daryl Porter, one of the players on Buffalo's kickoff team who made an
egregious error by vacating his coverage lane, thus allowing Kevin Dyson to take Frank
Wycheck's expertly deceptive lateral – that's what they called it in Tennessee, while in
Buffalo it was referred to as an illegal forward pass – and inconceivably scoot
untouched 75 yards for the winning touchdown.

"I still haven't gotten over it," Porter said, six months after the fact. "That will be
something that's in the back of my mind for the rest of my life."

It was quickly nicknamed the Music City Miracle, and it will live in NFL infamy,
right alongside the Franco Harris Immaculate Reception, as one of the most bizarre
plays in league history. But for the fans of Western New York, it was merely the Queen
City Nightmare, just another in a litany of tearjerkers they would have to endure.

"I don't know if it's the city of Buffalo or what it is, but it's just unbelievable. It's
a blue collar, hard-working city," defensive end Phil Hansen said, inferring that Western
New Yorkers simply didn't deserve the seemingly endless stream of bad sports luck.
"There was in the crease last year with the Sabres and they get screwed, and now this.
It's just unbelievable."

Buffalonians still hadn't gotten over the injustice of the previous spring when the

Sabres lost the sixth game of the NHL's Stanley Cup Finals to Dallas in triple overtime when the Stars' Brett Hull scored the Cup-clinching goal with one skate planted in the crease, a clear of violation of league rules.

And despite the passing of nearly a decade, the bleeding still hadn't stopped from Scott Norwood's Wide Right in Super Bowl 25. Throw in the other three Super Bowl losses, plus the 1998 game in New England when the zebras stole a victory from the Bills with some of the most pathetic officiating ever, and you get Hansen's point. No sports-loving city should have to burden so much heartbreak. But here Bills fans were again, lamenting another incredible loss, and this one broke new ground.

It had already been a chaotic week for the Bills leading up to the game. Buffalo had clinched a playoff berth in Week 16 and its position could not be altered positively or negatively in the season finale against Indianapolis, so coach Wade Phillips decided to rest starting quarterback Doug Flutie and give backup Rob Johnson some work.

Flutie had guided the Bills to 10 wins in 15 starts, but he had not been overly impressive, and when Johnson enjoyed a scintillating day in a blowout over the Colts, Phillips shocked the NFL nation by naming Johnson as his starter for the wild-card game at Tennessee's Adelphia Coliseum. As soon as the words left Phillips' mouth, Buffalo's simmering quarterback controversy transformed from the mellowness of a Kenny G concert to the madness of a Limp Bizkit show.

Phillips was skewered for the decision and the ever-competitive Flutie burned a silent rage, using every ounce of energy in his undersized

(Annette Lein/Rochester Democrat and Chronicle)

When the Bills lost to Tennessee in the 2000 playoff game that became known as the Music City Miracle, Eric Moulds caught three passes for 62 yards. Since then he has become Buffalo's primary offensive weapon..

body to not vent in public. As if a full-blown quarterback controversy wasn't enough, Andre Reed chose this week to write on his personal web site that he was unhappy with his role in the Buffalo offense and he hinted that he'd like to play for a new team in 2000. And then there was the issue of Buffalo's injury-riddled offensive line having to face Tennessee's frightening defense led by Super Freak Jevon Kearse at the Titans' new stadium where no visiting team had yet to win.

The game started poorly for Buffalo as Johnson was sacked by Kearse early in the second quarter and fumbled the ball out of the end zone for a safety. And after Derrick Mason returned the ensuing free kick 42 yards to the Buffalo 28, Steve McNair scored on a two-yard quarterback keeper five plays later for a 9-0 lead.

The margin grew to 12-0 when Al Del Greco – given a mulligan when his missed field goal attempt from 45 yards was nullified by a Buffalo penalty – kicked a 40-yarder on the final play of the first half.

The Bills looked like a beaten team as they jogged off the field, a team unable to overcome all of the negativity surrounding it. However, the game took an abrupt turn when Antowain Smith broke a 44-yard run on the first play from scrimmage in the second half, and he later scored on a four-yard jaunt to rejuvenate Buffalo's hopes.

The Buffalo defense – which limited the Titans to a meager 76 second-half yards – was now energized and McNair, Eddie George and company could not do anything. Meanwhile, early in the fourth quarter, Johnson directed a 65-yard drive, the key play his 37-yard pass to Eric Moulds, which set up Smith's one-yard touchdown plunge. The Bills' failed on a two-point conversion, but they led 13-12 with 11:08 remaining.

After an exchange of punts left Tennessee with possession at the Bills 45, the Titans were finally able to make some headway against the Buffalo defense as they advanced 27 yards, enabling Del Greco to kick a 36-yard field goal for a 15-13 lead with 1:48 to go.

Unfazed, Buffalo stormed back when Kevin Williams returned the kickoff 33 yards to the Bills 39 and Johnson went to work. He hit Peerless Price for 14 yards, Jonathan Linton ran for 12, and Johnson – despite losing his right shoe on a rollout – found Price on the sideline for nine yards to the Titans 23. With 20 seconds to go and no timeouts at his disposal, Phillips sent in Steve Christie to kick a go-ahead 41-yard field goal, and he delivered.

And then he and the rest of the Bills quivered.

"One minute we've won the game, then it's gone," said Christie. "I don't know what to say."

No one did.

After Christie's field goal, Titans coach Jeff Fisher gathered his kickoff return team and called for Home Run Throwback, a trick return that he said the Titans practiced every Saturday during the regular season. However, there was a hitch. Actually two. Mason was supposed to be the player near the sideline who would catch the lateral and run, but he had tweaked an ankle and was unavailable. His backup, Anthony

Dorsett, was battling cramps. So Fisher yelled for Dyson to get in the game.

"He just called my name out of the blue," said Dyson. "As we were running on the field they were trying to explain to me the gist of the play."

Dyson listened well.

Christie pooched the kickoff and Tennessee caught a break when Lorenzo Neal was able to field the ball cleanly at about the 25-yard-line, and he quickly handed it to Wycheck.

"We wanted to kick it high and short where they didn't have the timing on the play like if we kicked it deep," explained Phillips.

Said Christie: "You either pooch it or squib it so their prime returner doesn't get a

---

ERIC MOULDS

It was the end of the bitterly disappointing 1997 season, and just as the Bills were about to head their separate ways for the long off-season, Thurman Thomas looked over at Moulds in the locker room and said "You're going into your third year (in 1998). It's about time you turned your life around and start doing what it takes to play in this league."

Moulds, Buffalo's first-round draft choice in 1996, was looking like a bust two years into his NFL career. He had been unable to crack the starting lineup, and he made more news off the field than on it with charges that he had beaten a woman and was a deadbeat dad.

But heeding the veteran Thomas' words, Moulds worked out like a madman, came to training camp 15 pounds lighter, got his personal life in order, and enjoyed a breakout 1998 season catching 67 passes for a team-record 1,368 yards. Since then, he has been one of the most productive receivers in the NFL and two Pro Bowl appearances serve as the proof.

One NFL scout, asked to assess the league's best receivers in 2002, said "Give me Eric Moulds and Marvin Harrison (Colts). I can win with those guys."

Bills quarterback Drew Bledsoe tends to agree. Bledsoe drools when he talks about Moulds' impressive combination of strength, speed and big-play ability.

"Eric is the most explosive, the most powerful and the strongest receiver I've ever played with," Bledsoe said. "I throw the ball and just stand back and watch, because I know he's going to do something amazing."

---

chance to set up a proper return, but they got it to him anyway."

That's because the Bills' coverage team, like magnets drawn to steel, converged on Wycheck thinking he would just run up the gut as far as he could to give Tennessee one or two cracks at a Hail Mary pass. This calamitous maneuver left Buffalo's right flank wide open, and the Titans couldn't believe their good fortune. Wycheck threw a 30-yard sideways lateral out to Dyson, and when Dyson looked up, he had nothing but

75 yards of brownish-green grass and a few of his teammates serving as escorts in front of him. He pranced all the way to the end zone, crossing the goal line for the winning points with three seconds remaining, the roar from the crowd louder than if the Concorde at landed at midfield.

"The guy threw it back and the guys on that side broke down, they should have stayed over there, but they didn't," said Phillips. "I've seen a lot of them, but I haven't seen one like that."

"I was ready to commit suicide," said Titans general manager Floyd Reese of his mood after Christie's field goal. "Then the next thing I know I'm dancing on the table."

And the Bills – after a lengthy instant replay review to determine the legality of the lateral – were staring at the sky in disbelief, trying to figure out what had just happened.

"I wasn't on the field, but if I was I probably would have been suckered like everybody else so don't let me lie to you," said Wiley, who left the Bills to sign a lucrative free agent contract with San Diego following the 2000 season. "I've never gotten over it. It felt like *Alice in Wonderland* – you just did not believe this was happening. As I'm watching I wanted to push pause so the whole world would stop."

In the weeks that followed, the heartbreak and frustration mounted for the Bills as the Titans went on the road to defeat Indianapolis in the divisional round and Jacksonville in the AFC Championship Game to reach Super Bowl 34. "As long as there was an NFL game on, especially the ones Tennessee was in, it hurt bad to watch," said Wiley. That's because the Bills were convinced they were the better team, and they felt they would have duplicated Tennessee's run through the playoffs and wound up opposite St. Louis in the Super Bowl. "They knew it and we knew it, we should have won that game, but you can't say that when you look at the scoreboard," said Porter. "Just seeing those guys go that far, to see the team that beat us go to the Super Bowl, we can say we lost to a Super Bowl team, but on the other hand, it should have been us."

Bibliography

The following newspapers, magazines, wire services, web sites and books were used to research the stories contained within this collection:

NEWSPAPERS and MAGAZINES

The Buffalo News
Buffalo Courier-Express
Rochester Democrat and Chronicle
Rochester Times-Union
Olean Times Herald
USA Today
The Washington Post
The New York Times
Sports Illustrated
Kitchener-Waterloo Record
The Toronto Sun
The Toronto Star
St. Louis Post-Dispatch
Colorado Springs Gazette Telegraph
The Denver Post
Fort-Lauderdale Sun-Sentinel
The Miami Herald
The Boston Globe
The Montreal Gazette
Dallas Morning News
The Milwaukee Journal
The San Francisco Chronicle
The Tennessean
Newsday
Denver Rocky Mountain News

WIRE SERVICES and WEB SITES

The Associated Press
United Press International
Canadian Press
Buffalobills.com
Indians.com

Bibliography

WIRE SERVICES and WEB SITES *Cont'd*

Bisons.com
BaseballLibrary.com
BaseballReference.com
NFL.com

BOOKS

*Relentless - The Hard-Hitting History of
Buffalo Bills Football,* by Sal Maiorana

*The Buffalo Bills and the Almost-Dream
Season,* by Vic Carucci

By A Nose, by Fred Smerlas and Vic Carucci

Heaven and Hell in the NHL, by Punch
Imlach with Scott Young

*Sabres: 26 Seasons in Buffalo's Memorial
Auditorium,* by Ross Brewitt

*Celebrate the Tradition - A History of the
Buffalo Sabres,* by Budd Bailey

The History of Baseball, by Allison Danzig
and Joe Reichler

O.J. Simpson - Football's Record Rusher,
by Larry Felser

The Great Gretzky, by Terry Jones
Gretzky, by Rick Reilly

*Thank You Sabres - Memories of the
1972-73 Season,* by Sal Maiorana

The 100 Seasons of Buffalo Baseball, by
Joe Overfield

*Banks to Sandberg to Grace - Five
Decades of Love and Frustration
with the Chicago Cubs,* by Carrie Muskat.

Birth of a Publishing Company

The Buffalo area's most innovative publishing will celebrate its 20th anniversary in 2004 by hitting a benchmark that few regional publishing houses achieve. By that time, Western New York Wares Inc. will have moved more than 175,000 books and other regional products into homes, schools and libraries around the world.

If all these books were laid cover-to-cover starting at the foot of Main Street near HSBC Center, the trail would stretch past the UB South Campus, snake through Williamsville, Clarence and end way past Akron Falls Park! Putting it a different way, we've printed and distributed nearly 20 million pages of information about our region.

A pretty impressive path for a company that sprouted its roots in trivial turf!

The year was 1984 and the trivia craze was taking the nation by storm. As Buffalo journalist Brian Meyer played a popular trivia game with friends in his North Buffalo living room, he envisioned a game that tests players' knowledge about people and events in their hometown. Western New York Trivia Quotient sold out its first edition in six weeks and established Meyer as an up-and-coming young entrepreneur.

A year later, he compiled a book of quotations that chronicled the feisty reign of Mayor Jimmy Griffin. Meyer refuses to disclose how many six-packs were consumed while sifting through hundreds of "Griffinisms."

Meyer, a City Hall reporter for the Buffalo News, spent 15 years at WBEN Radio where he served a managing editor. As founder and president of Western New York Wares Inc., Meyer has collaborated with dozens of authors, artists and photographers. By 2003, the region's premier publisher of local books had been involved in publishing, marketing or distributing more than 100 regional products.

The Buffalo native is a graduate of the Marquette University, St. Joseph's Collegiate Institute and Buffalo Public School #56. He teaches communications courses at Buffalo State College and Medaille College. Meyer is treasurer of the Greater Buffalo Society of Professional Journalists' Scholarship Fund.

Meyer is assisted by Michele Ratzel, the company's business manager, and Tom Connolly, manager of marketing and distribution. The trio has nearly 45 years of cumulative experience in regional publishing. Connolly works as a news anchor and producer at WBEN Radio. He co-authored *Hometown Heroes: Western New Yorkers in Desert Storm*. Ratzel works at the Park School of Buffalo.

Other Regional Books

Visit our Web site at _www.buffalobooks.com_ for a complete list of titles distributed by Western New York Wares Inc.

Tale of the Tape: A History of the Buffalo Bills From the Inside – Eddie "Abe" Abramoski reflects on scores on humorous, emotional and enlightening anecdotes that stretch back to the first Bills training camp in East Aurora. Many photos accompany the lively text.
ISBN: 1-879201-41-0 $10.95

Bodyslams in Buffalo: The Complete History of Pro Wrestling In Western New York – Author Dan Murphy traces the region's rich wrestling history, from Ilio DiPaolo and Dick "The Destroyer" Beyer, to Adorable Adrian Adonis. Dozens of photos.
ISBN: 1-879201-42-9 $9.95

Buffalo Memories: Gone But Not Forgotten -- The late George Kunz was blessed with a phenomenal memory. In his later years, he began chronicling his recollections of his Depression upbringing. For years, his anecdotes on everything from Bisons' games at Offermann Stadium to rides on the Canadiana and shopping excursions to 998 Broadway graced the pages of the Buffalo News. This book is a collection of about 200 of these anecdotes.
ISBN: 0-9671480-9-X $15.00

Haunted Places of Western New York – Mason Winfield, the region's most high-profile paranormal investigator and 21st century "ghosthunter," pens a first-of-a-kind guidebook. Readers learn about "spooky communities" in the area, encountering haunted inns, highways, colleges and theaters. There are even chapters that focus on battlefield ghosts and grave haunts.
ISBN: 1-879201-45-3 $12.95

Spirits of the Great Hill: More Haunted Sites and Ancient Mysteries of Upstate New York --
From Mark Twain's Buffalo ghost, to Houdini's Halloween, Mason Winfield pens a riveting sequel to his supernatural survey of the region.
ISBN: 1-879201-35-6 $13.95

Shadows of the Western Door: Haunted Sites and Ancient Mysteries of Upstate New York – A supernatural safari across Western New York. Guided by the insights of modern research, author Mason Winfield pens a colorful, provocative and electrifying study of the paranormal.
ISBN: 1-829201-22-4 $13.95

A Ghosthunter's Journal: Tales of the Supernatural and the Strange in Upstate New York
A delightfully diverse smorgasbord of strange encounters, all of them set in Western New York. The 13 fictional stories are inspired by the files of Mason Winfield.
ISBN: 1-879201-29-1 $12.95

Victorian Buffalo: Images From the Buffalo and Erie County Public Library –
Visit Buffalo as it looked in the 19th century through steel engravings, woodcuts, lithography and other forms of
nonphotographic art. Author Cynthia VanNess has selected scenes that showcase everyday life and views of historic structures created by luminaries like Frank Lloyd Wright, Louis Sullivan and E.B. Green.
ISBN: 1-879201-30-5 $13.95

The Erie Canal: The Ditch That Opened a Nation -- Despite its shallow depths, the waters of the Erie
carry an amazing history legacy. It was in canal towns like Lockport and Tonawanda where the doors to the
American frontier were unlocked. Written by Daniel T. Murphy, the book includes dozens of photos.
ISBN: 1-879201-34-8 $8.95

Erie Canal Legacy: Architectural Treasures of the Empire State -- Photographer Andy Olenick and
author Richard O. Reisem take readers on a 363-mile journey along the canal route. This hardcover book is
comprised of full-color photos and an enlightening text.
ISBN: 0-9641706-6-3 $39.95

National Landmarks of Western New York: Famous People and Historic Places -- Gracious mansions and thundering waterfalls. Battleships and nostalgic fireboats. Power plants and Indian long houses. Author
Jan Sheridan researched nearly 30 National Historic Landmarks in the Buffalo-Niagara and Finger Lakes
regions. Dozens of photographs, maps and an index.
ISBN: 1-879201-36-4 $9.95

**Beyond Buffalo: A Photographic Journey and Guide to the Secret Natural Wonders of our
Region** – Full color photographs and informative vignettes showcase 30 remarkable sites. Author David Reade
also includes directions and tips for enjoying each site.
ISBN: 1-879201-19-4 $19.95

Western New York Weather Guide – Readers won't want any "winteruptions" as they breeze through this
lively book written by former Channel 7 weather guru Tom Jolls. Co-authored by Brian Meyer and Joseph
VanMeer, the book focuses on historic and humorous weather events over the past century.
ISBN: 1-879201-18-1 $7.95

White Death: Blizzard of '77 – This 356-page softcover book chronicles one of the region's most dramatic
historical events. Written by Erno Rossi, the book includes more than 60 photographs.
ISBN: 0-920926-03-7 $16.95

Great Lake Effects: Buffalo Beyond Winter and Wings – a unique cookbook that is filled with intriguing historical facts about the region. The hardcover book has been compiled by the Junior League of Buffalo.
ISBN: 1-879201-18-1 $18.95

Buffalo Treasures: A Downtown Walking Guide – Readers are led on a fascinating tour of 25 major
buildings. A user-friendly map and dozens of illustrations by Kenneth Sheridan supplement an enlightening text
by Jan Sheridan.
ISBN: 1-879201-15-1 $4.95

Church Tales of the Niagara Frontier: Legends, History & Architecture – This first-of-a-kind book traces the rich history and folklore of the region through accounts of 60 area churches and places of worship. Written by the late Austin M. Fox and illustrated by Lawrence McIntyre.
ISBN : 1-879201-13-5 $14.95

Symbol & Show: The Pan-American Exposition of 1901 -- A riveting look at perhaps the greatest event in Buffalo's history. Written by the late Austin M. Fox and illustrated by Lawrence McIntyre, this book offers a lively assessment of the Exposition, bringing to light many half-forgotten facts.
ISBN: 1-879201-33-X $15.95

Frank Lloyd Wright's Darwin D. Martin House: Rescue of a Landmark-- The untold story of the abandonment and rescue of the region's most architecturally-significant home is recounted in vivid detail by Marjorie L. Quinlan. The book includes color photos and detailed architectural plans.
ISBN: 1-879201-32-1 $13.95

Buffalo's Brush With the Arts: From Huck Finn to Murphy Brown – A fascinating adventure behind the manuscripts and million-dollar book deals, highlighting the Niagara Frontier's connection to many creative geniuses. Authored by Joe Marren, the book contains more than 20 photographs from the Courier-Express Collection.
ISBN: 1-879201-24-0 $7.95

Classic Buffalo: A Heritage of Distinguished Architecture -- A stunning hardcover book pays tribute to the region's architectural heritage. Striking full-color photographs by Andy Olenick and an engaging text by Richard O. Reisem make this coffee-table book a keepsake for history buffs.
ISBN: 0-9671480-06 $39.95

Uncrowned Queens: African American Women Community Builders of Western New York. Historians Peggy Brooks-Bertram and Dr. Barbara Seals Nevergold celebrate the accomplishments of African American women. Some of them are well-known; others have not received previous recognition.
ISBN: 0-9722977-0-7 $11.95

Buffalo's Waterfront : A Guidebook – Edited by Tim Tielman, this user-friendly guide showcases more than 100 shoreline sites. It includes a handy fold-out map. Published by the Preservation Coalition of Erie County.
ISBN: 1-879201-00-3 $5.95

 The Rainbow City: Celebrating Light, Color and Architecture at the Pan-American Exposition, Buffalo 1901 -- The story of Buffalo's glorious moment, recounted in 160 pages and more than 20 images. Written by Kerry S. Grant of the University at Buffalo, the book chronicles an era when Buffalo was the nation's eighth largest city.
ISBN: 0-9671480-5-7 $39.95

Goat Island: Niagara's Scenic Retreat – Historian Paul Gromosiak explores the people, attractions, animals and plants that makes the islands above Niagara Falls a fascinating destination. The book includes color photos and a detailed map.
ISBN: 1-879201-43-7 $9.95

Nature's Niagara: A Walk on the Wild Side – Learn more about the wild animals, plants and geological formations at Niagara Falls. Written by Paul Gromosiak, the book includes many full-color photographs and maps.
ISBN: 1-879201-31-3 $8.95

Daring Niagara: 50 Death-Defying Stunts at the Falls
Paul Gromosiak pens a heart-stopping adventure about those who barreled, boated, even bicycled to fame. The book includes vintage photos.
ISBN: 1-879201-23-2 $6.95

Niagara Falls Q&A: Answers to the 100 Most Common Questions About Niagara Falls. -- Author Paul Gromosiak spent four summers chatting with 40,000 Falls tourists. This invaluable guide answers 100 commonly-asked questions. The book also includes photos, many of them in color.
ISBN: 0-9620314-8-8 $4.50

Water Over the Falls: 101 of the Most Memorable Events at Niagara Falls
Daredevils who defied the Mighty Niagara. Tragic rock slides and heroic rescues. More than 100 true-to-life tales are chronicled by local historian Paul Gromosiak. Color photos and vintage black-and-white photos.
ISBN: 1-879201-16-X $8.99

Zany Niagara: The Funny Things People Say About Niagara Falls
A lighthearted tour of humorous happenings and historical oddities. Penned by Paul Gromosiak and illustrated by John Hardiman.
ISBN: 1-879201-06-2 $4.95

Exploring Niagara: The Complete Guide to Niagara Falls and Vicinity
Filled with 77 spectacular full-color photos, the guide includes dozens of wineries, canals, waterfalls and mansions. Authors Hans and Allyson Tammemagi also chronicle the history that shaped the region.
ISBN: 0-9681815-0-3 $14.25

Niagara Falls
One of the world's most spectacular natural wonders springs to life in a book that contains more than 150 color photographs. From a visit in 1678 when a missionary recorded the first eyewitness account of the Falls, to an autumn day in 1993 when Dave Mundy became the only person to survive two barrel rides over the Niagara, readers experience an exhilarating tour. The book includes chapters on the Gorge, Niagara-on-the-Lake, wineries, the famous floral clock and Fort Erie.
ISBN: 2-84339-023-0 $9.99

The Magic of Niagara
Viewing the Mighty Niagara for the first time stirs images of tranquility, power and magic. The story of Niagara is 12,000 years old, and author George Bailey skillfully captures the historical highlights in a book that contains a riveting text and more than 100 photographs. Sections include
Niagara in the winter, the Maid of the Mist, famous daredevils and the Niagara Parks Butterfly Conservancy.
ISBN: 0-9682635-0-X $15.99

This is Niagara Falls
Vibrant color photographs – more than 50 of them – capture the power and majesty of the Mighty Niagara. From the moment when darkness descends on this wonder and a dazzling display of lights appears, to the instant when the Maid of the Boat inches close to the foamy base of the Falls, this book captures the mystique of a this natural wonder.
ISBN: 1-879201-38-0 $7.98

Toronto and Niagara Falls
Two world-renowned destinations are showcased in one photo-packed book! More than 240 full-color photographs, a detailed street map, informative text and user-friendly index make this an invaluable companion. Readers will explore Chinatown, museums, forts and gardens in Toronto. The Niagara Falls section highlights such attractions as Cave of the Winds and Maid of the Mist.
ISBN: 88-8029-569-1 $15.99

Please include 8.25% sales tax for all orders in New York. Also include shipping charges:
Orders under $25... $3; $25-$49... $4.00; $50-more... $5.00.
Visit our Web site at: www.buffalobooks.com or write for a catalog:

Western New York Wares Inc.
P.O. Box 733
Ellicott Station
Buffalo, New York 14205